A Textbook of Biomedical Laboratory Techniques

A Textbook of Biomedical Laboratory Techniques

P. Venkatesan

Published by
ATLANTIC
PUBLISHERS & DISTRIBUTORS (P) LTD
7/22, Ansari Road, Darya Ganj,
New Delhi-110002
Phones : +91-11-40775252, 23273880, 23275880, 23280451
Fax : +91-11-23285873
Web : www.atlanticbooks.com
E-mail : orders@atlanticbooks.com

Branch Office
5, Nallathambi Street, Wallajah Road,
Chennai-600002
Phones : +91-44-64611085, 32413319
E-mail : chennai@atlanticbooks.com

Printed in India at Nice Printing Press, A-33/3A, Site-IV, Industrial Area, Sahibabad, Ghaziabad, U.P.

Preface

Biomedical laboratory involves a variety of distinct disciplines. However, it can be conveniently grouped under two major headings, namely 'Conventional laboratory techniques', and 'Modern laboratory techniques'.

Laboratory medicine is the supporting science, which includes many basic techniques without which diagnosis, treatment and management of illness being suffered by the patients cannot be made by a medical doctor even in these modern days in developed as well as developing countries like India. The phenomenal growth of paramedical science or laboratory medicine today would not have been possible without these basic techniques.

A Textbook of Biomedical Laboratory Techniques aims at providing some basic and relevant information on important biomedical laboratory techniques with illustrations on haematology, serology, blood bank techniques, urine, sputum, seminal fluid and motion analyses, histopathological techniques, immunodiagnostic techniques, etc.

This book is written in as concise and simple a manner as possible with a view to helping the students, technicians and teachers in various dimensions of biomedical laboratories in universities, colleges and hospitals. I am highly thankful to Dr. G. Surendra Babu, Senior Consultant Physician, Keerthana Nursing Home, Trichy, Tamil Nadu for having provided critical suggestions to my script. I dedicate this volume to my mentor—late Dr. T.K. Raghunatha Rao who was instrumental in my growth and development in the field of laboratory techniques.

P. Venkatesan

Contents

1

Haematology

1.1 Reading of Blood Pressure

Aim: To determine the blood pressure of a person.

Materials required: Sphygmomanometer and Stethoscope.

(Sphygmomanometer consists of a rubber bag covered with a cloth envelope, which is wrapped around the upper arm over the brachial artery, at an approximate distance of two finger breath. One rubber tube connects the inside of the bag with a manometer containing mercury. Another tube connects the inside of the bag to a hand operated rubber bulb with a release valve.)

Principle: Blood pressure is measured and maintained constant by regulation of water and salt in the blood. As the blood is pumped rapidly along the arteries by the heart, the pressure in the heart and in the peripheral vessels varies depending upon the distance traversed by the blood. When the external pressure around the arm of a person is increased than the blood pressure, the blood flow is arrested in the arteries. By decreasing the pressure, the sudden flow of blood is initiated. When it is decreased further, it becomes normal as that of pulsating flow. This variation indicates the systolic and diastolic pressures of the person. This can be monitored with the stethoscope.

Blood pressure (in mm/Hg) = Cardiac output × Peripheral resistance

Procedure: The pressure pad of the Sphygmomanometer is tied around the upper arm at the left hand of the person. Care is taken to place the end bulb of the pad along the inner side of the arm. With the help of pressure bulb, the pad is inflated, with the air nozzle being kept closed. The increase in pressure is noted in the meter scale, against the mercury column. By regulating the air nozzle, the pressure is gradually released. The diaphragm of the stethoscope is placed along the brachial artery position.

Appearance of sound, known as "Korotkoff's sound" is noted as systolic blood pressure and the disappearance of sound is noted as diastolic blood pressure. The initial continuous flow of blood is increased and recorded in terms of systolic pressure. The seizure of the "Gur" sound and initiation of normal beat indicates the diastolic pressure and at that time the pressure gauge should not be disturbed. The arm should be placed straight on the table to ensure easy flow of blood.

Normal value: Systolic : 120 mm/Hg
Diastolic: 80 mm/Hg

Clinical significance: Hypertension is the condition when the blood pressure is more than 130/80 mm/Hg. It may be due to increased blood output or increased heart rate. Once high blood pressure is diagnosed, a lifelong monitoring and treatment become necessary. The external factors that alter the pressure are age, increase in the level of sodium and/or potassium, high fat intake, obesity, smoking and environmental stress. The internal factors are stress, inheritance, pheochromocytoma, Cushing's syndrome, intracranial tumours and primary aldosteronism.

The pathological changes accompanied by hypertension are thickening of the arterioles with hyaline materials and later hypertrophy of the myocardium of the left ventricle. Moderate hypertension eventually leads to cardiac failure with congestion of the pulmonary and systemic veins. It also causes ischaemic changes in the kidney and nephrosclerosis. Pregnancy also causes hypertension. The two methods of recording blood pressure in human are ascultatory method and palpatory method.

1.2 Bleeding Time

Aim: To determine the bleeding time of a person.

Materials required: Rectified spirit, fine needle, cotton, blotting paper and stop clock.

Principle: The bleeding time is the time required for the capillary blood to stop bleeding from the region of injury in the finger.

Procedure: The finger or the ear lobe is rubbed firmly to ensure adequate blood supply and is then sterilized with the surgical spirit. With the sterilized and disposable lancet, the tip of the finger or the ear lobe is punctured. As soon as the punctured region starts bleeding, the stop clock is started. With the help of the blotting paper, the overflowing blood is removed once in 15 seconds without touching the skin. The punctured region is pressed gently and periodically until the last drop of blood is removed. When the blood flow stops, the stop clock is switched off and the time is noted.

Normal value: 2–6 minutes.

Clinical significance: Determination of bleeding time recognizes vascular defect and platelet disorder. Prolonged bleeding time is generally found with:

a. Primary or Idiopathic Thrombocytopenic Purpura (platelet count less than 50,000/µl) and platelet dysfunction.

b. Secondary Thrombocytopenic Purpura
   i. Dengue Haemorrhagic fever
   ii. Bacterial endocarditis
   iii. Drug induced.

Due to the deficiency of coagulation factor VIII, bleeding time will be high with a normal platelet count. The other methods for the determination of bleeding time are Duke method and Ivy method.

1.3 Clotting Time

Aim: To determine the clotting time of a person.

Materials required: Rectified spirit, disposable lancet, cotton, non-heparinised capillary tube (10 cm long × 0.8 to 1.2 mm diameter) and stop clock.

Principle: When the blood is exposed to atmospheric air, due to thrombin reaction, fibrin formation occurs. The reaction takes place in continuation of bleeding and in the presence of coagulation factors. Normal clotting time follows the bleeding time.

Procedure: The finger is prepared for a capillary blood extraction. With the help of a sterile disposable lancet, an incision is made to a depth of 3 mm. As soon as the finger bleeds, the stop clock is started. The first drop of blood is wiped off and then the blood is allowed to enter the capillary tube leaving some portion on either tips. Trapping of air bubbles in the capillary tube should be avoided. The capillary tube is then broken for every 15 seconds. When a thin string of fibrin appears between the broken ends of the capillary tube, the stop clock is stopped and the time is noted.

Normal values: 3–7 minutes.

Clinical significance: The interval between the appearance of the first drop of blood on the finger followed by loading the blood in the capillary tube and the appearance of fibrin is known as the clotting time. Deficiency of coagulation factors such as ionic calcium, vitamin K, fibrinogen, thromboplastin, anti-haemophilic factors are recognized by this method. In the case of prolonged clotting time, the patient should be subjected to more detailed tests for the identification of the causal factor. Presence of circulating anti-coagulant like heparin and genetic disorders such as Haemophilia (Bleeder's/Royal disease due to the expression of sex linked recessive genes) will also cause abnormal and prolonged clotting time. This procedure is, therefore, of immense importance to monitor heparin therapy.

1.4 Estimation of Haemoglobin Concentration

Aim: To estimate the concentration of haemoglobin in the blood of a human.

Materials required: Surgical spirit, cotton, sterile lancet, Sahli's pipette, colorimeter, Drabkin's solution and serum tubes.

Principle: Haemoglobin in the blood can be estimated by Cyanomethaemoglobin method. It is a colorimetric procedure for determining haemoglobin concentration. An aliquot of well-mixed coagulated blood or capillary blood is taken and reacted with the Drabkin's solution. This chemical reaction yields a product of stable colour. The intensity of the colour is proportional to the haemoglobin concentration and obeys Beer's law.

Reagents

1. **Drabkin's solution:** 50 mg Potassium cyanide and 50 mg Potassium ferricyanide are mixed well and dissolved in 1000 ml of distilled water. This reagent should be stored only at room temperature in a brown bottle or kept in darkness; otherwise decolouration is possible due to the reduction of ferricyanide.
2. **Cyanomethaemoglobin (Standard):** This is commercially available or may be obtained from a reference laboratory.

Specimen: EDTA (Ethylene Diamine Tetra Acetic acid) anticoagulated venous blood or capillary blood can also be used directly.

Procedure: The serum tubes have to be labelled as blank, test and standard. Five ml of Drabkin's solution has to be pipetted into each of these tubes. Mouth pipetting must be avoided since the reagent is highly toxic. The finger has to be sterilized with surgical spirit and air dried before using the lancet. The capillary blood is collected up to 20 µl of Sahli's pipette and replaced with 20 µl of Drabkin's solution from the serum tube. The same method is followed while adding 20 µl of distilled water in the tube marked 'blank' and standard in the tube marked for it. Precaution must be taken to take exactly 20 µl and not otherwise in order to avoid error in the value. The content is mixed well twice and kept at room temperature for 10 minutes. Meanwhile the colorimeter is switched on and warmed up for 10 minutes. The wavelength is set for 540 nm or a suitable filter in this range. The instrument has to be standardized by setting zero with the control knob. With the blank (B) prepared, the instrument has to be set for 100. Then the standard solution (S) has to be fed in the colorimeter to read the absorbance value on the scale. The procedure is repeated with the test solution (T). Acid haematin method, specific gravity method and spectrophotometric method are the other methods used for the determination of haemoglobin.

Normal value: Male : 14–17 gm/dl

Female : 13–15 gm/dl

Formula

$$\text{Haemoglobin g/dl} = \frac{\text{Absorbance of the test solution}}{\text{Absorbance of the standard solution}} \times 100$$

Clinical significance: A decrease in haemoglobin concentration in blood below normal value is a sign of anaemia, which is lower in adult woman compared to man. Particularly, the value decreases during pregnancy due to haemodilution.

Types of anaemia

1. **Iron deficiency anaemia:** About 75 per cent of iron in our body is present in haemoglobin. A certain amount of iron is also present as myoglobin. A man with an average body weight of 70 kg has about 4.5 grams of total body iron. Iron deficiency occurs when there is a blood loss, a period of rapid growth such as adolescent period or when a woman is pregnant. Certain diseases such as celiac disease, sprue and mal-absorption syndrome affect the absorption of iron. Achlorhydria and Gastric surgery reduce the area of absorption of iron. Vitamin B complex and protein deficiency are associated with symptoms when malnutrition is the cause of ID anaemia.
2. **Pernicious anaemia:** This is due to the inability in absorbing vitamin B_{12} from the intestine. It is also caused by Autoimmune gastritis, leading to a condition

called 'achlorhydria'. Lack of appetite, mild lemon discolouration of the skin and beefy red tongue are vital symptoms of pernicious anaemia. It is also called Megaloblastic Anaemia.

3. **Folic acid deficiency anaemia:** This vitamin is necessary for the bone marrow to make red blood cells. This type of megaloblastic anaemia occurs very frequently in pregnant women, in the elderly and in alcoholics due to poor diets. Certain chronic diseases such as steatorrhoea, sprue and abnormality of absorption in the intestine due to some drugs (e.g., anticonvulsants for the treatment of epilepsy) can cause deficiency of folic acid in the body. Breathlessness, tiredness and depression are the major symptoms of folic acid deficiency.
4. **Haemolytic anaemia:** The accelerated break down of red blood cells before its normal lifespan is known as haemolysis. Since large amount of haemoglobin gets released from the broken down cells that circulate as bilirubin, it results in Hyperbilirubinemia. Autoimmunity, mismatched blood transfusion, drugs and toxins produce Haemolytic anaemia.
5. **Sphaerocytosis:** It is a rare genetic defect in some individuals with a bone marrow that produces an excess of spherical RBC, a condition called sphaerocytosis. Since such cells are easily haemolysed, anaemia develops, the spleen enlarges and the bile gets overloaded, resulting in jaundice. In some cases, it also results in the formation of gall stones. The cure for this disorder is a simple one namely removal of spleen.
6. **G6PD Deficiency anaemia:** This is another rare genetic defect in the body leading to the deficiency of glucose 6–phosphate dehydrogenase. It has a sex linked inheritance pattern and it mainly affects males. This deficiency is usually called as Favism. Eating broad beans (*Vicia fava*), drugs such as phenocetin, sulphonamide or Quinidine and infections may cause

haemolysis leading to fever, dark urine, intense fatigue and jaundice.

7. **Sickle cell anaemia:** This is also a genetic disorder, in which red cells containing much abnormal haemoglobin become increasingly sickle shaped. If affected individuals are exposed to a low oxygen environment, there is an increased tendency for the sickle cells to block small blood vessels causing "Crisis".
8. **Thalassaemia:** This is a commonly inherited type of haemoglobin abnormality. In this type, there is an impaired ability to make normal haemoglobin. Removal of spleen, constant treatment with folic acid, periodic blood transfusion and pneumococcal vaccination help them live longer.
9. **Aplastic anaemia:** When the bone marrow fails due to poisoning, damage or replacement, this anaemia prevails. There is a likelihood of death in 6 months. Signs and symptoms are not usually noticeable. Breathlessness, fatigue and pallor are the signs of this anaemia. Bleeding gum and bruising are also prevailing symptoms. Bone marrow transplantation is the best alternative to cure this disorder. An increase in haemoglobin concentration occurs in Polycythemia vera rubra and congenital cyanotic heart diseases.

1.5 Determination of Haematocrit (Packed Cell Volume)

Aim: To determine the Packed cell volume by micro-haematocrit method.

Materials required: Cotton, spirit lamp, rectified spirit, sterile syringe and needle, centrifuge and Wintrobe's tube.

Principle: The erythrocytes or red blood cell volume of blood is determined by means of haematocrit i.e., the percentage of volume of the blood sample contributed by its packed cell volume. This determination involves the use of very well defined conditions notably by the dimensions of the tube in which the blood is placed and centrifuge force which is applied for a specific time to separate the plasma and cell fractions.

Procedure: The venous blood is withdrawn into a duly sterile hypodermic syringe by vein puncture. The blood is expelled into a serum tube or a bottle containing anticoagulant after removing the needle. The serum tube is inverted gently 10-20 times to ensure mixing of the anti-coagulant and blood. The oxalated blood is taken and mixed thoroughly by repeated inversion and is filled in Wintrobe's tube up to 100 mark. It is then centrifuged at 2500 rpm for 30 minutes. The original column of blood in the tube is 100 mm. The volume of packed cells can be read directly as percentage. Another method for determination of haematocrit is microhaematocrit method.

Microhaematocrit: This method requires only a small volume of specimen and hence it is ideal for skin puncture and for a limited amount of specimen. It also requires disposable capillary tubes, special centrifuge and reading device. Blood specimen is filled in heparinised capillary tube and sealed with soft wax. Two haematocrit tubes are placed in the radial grooves of the centrifuge head exactly opposite to each other and centrifuged at high speed (10,000 rpm) for 5 minutes. The capillary tube layers, viz., top is the clear plasma, middle is the thin layer of the buffy coat and bottom is the column of red cells. Haematocrit reader is used for finding out the value of haematocrit for each sample.

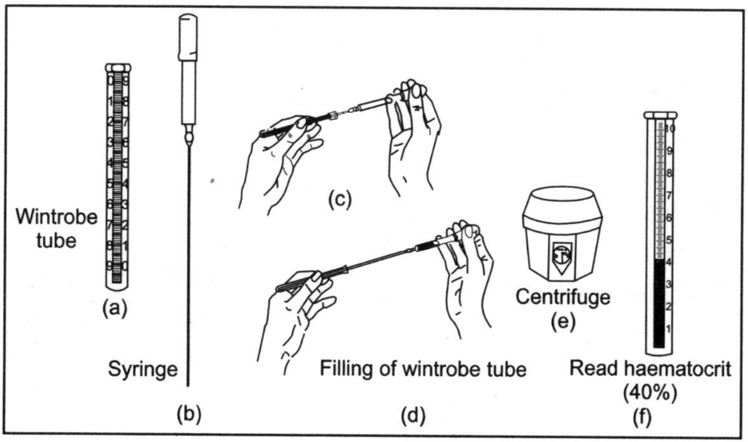

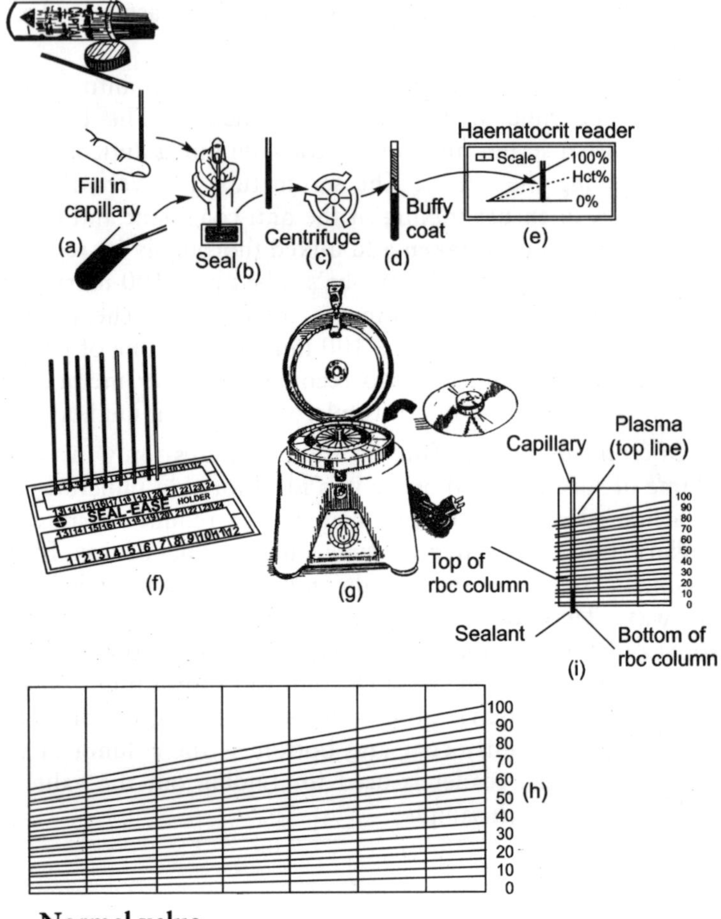

Normal value

Male	:	40–54%
Female	:	36–47%
Children	:	35–37.5%
Infants	:	44–62%

Clinical significance: Haematocrit (packed cell volume) is the amount of packed red cells following centrifugation, expressed as percentage of the total blood volume. Fall of haematocrit value may result from hydraemia (excessive fluid in the blood as occurring in pregnancy). An increase in haematocrit value indicates an increase in red cell production which occurs as a result of decrease of oxygen supply (congenital heart disease, emphysema) or as a malignant condition (Polycythemia). Elevated blood glucose and sodium may also produce elevated haematocrit because of the swelling of erythrocytes. Certain factors that alter the erythrocyte count are haemodilution and dehydration. Abnormalities in RBC size and extremely increased WBC may alter haematocrit value. As in the haemoglobin value, a decrease in haematocrit is a suitable measurement for detection of anaemia. It is useful to monitor the rehydration during the treatment of Dengue Haemorrhagic fever.

1.6 Differential Leucocyte Count (DLC)

Aim: To make the differential leucocytes count in human blood.

Materials required: Rectified spirit, cotton, lancet, glass slide, Leishmann's stain, buffer solution, staining tray and compound microscope.

Principle: Differential count represents the per cent distribution of various white blood cells in the peripheral blood. It is determined from a blood smear stained with a polychromic stain. In addition to differential count, microscopic study of blood smear helps to get an overall picture of the blood. Three major steps are involved in differential count namely, (i) preparation of smear, (ii) staining of the smear, (iii) microscopic observation.

The polychromic stain induces the multiple colours when applied to the blood cells. The stain gets dissolved in methanol and then buffered to the pH nearing 7. Methanol acts as a fixative and does not allow any further change in the cells. Due to the staining, the basic components of leucocytes are stained by the acidic eosin dye and they are described as eosinophilic (as acidophilic). When acidic components of the cells take blue to purple shade due to the basic dye called methylene blue, they are called basophilic. The neutral components of the cells are probably stained by both the dyes.

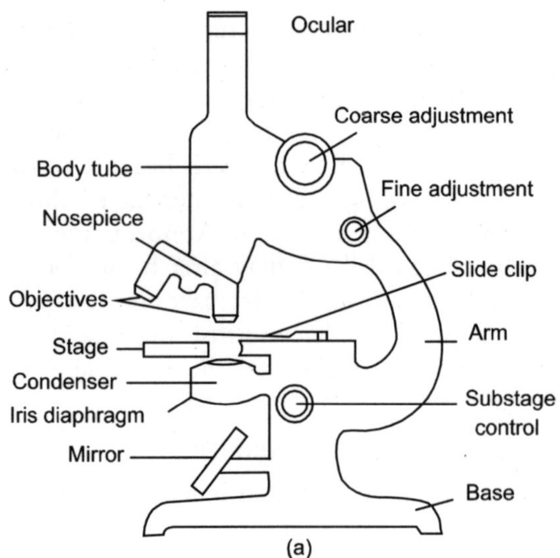
Ocular
Coarse adjustment
Body tube
Fine adjustment
Nosepiece
Slide clip
Objectives
Arm
Stage
Condenser
Iris diaphragm
Substage control
Mirror
Base

(a)

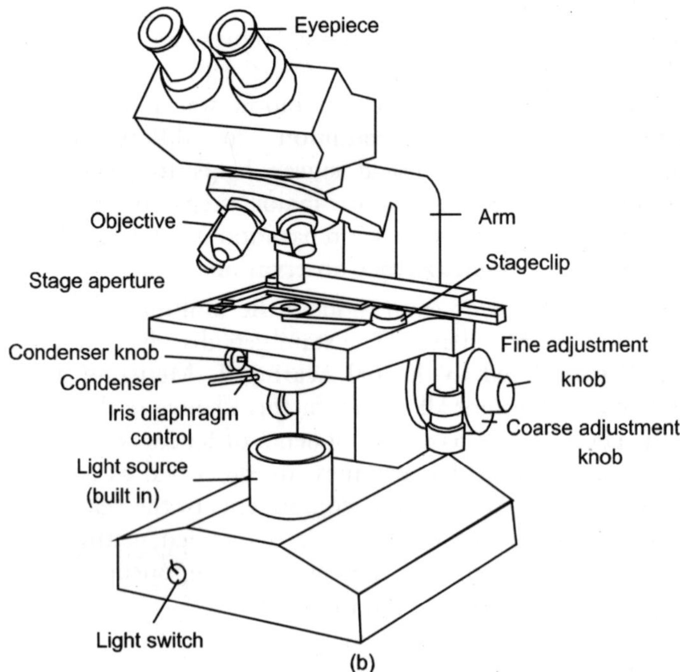
Eyepiece
Objective
Arm
Stageclip
Stage aperture
Condenser knob
Fine adjustment knob
Condenser
Iris diaphragm control
Coarse adjustment knob
Light source (built in)
Light switch

(b)

Preparation of Leishmann's stain: Methylene blue—1 gm; 0.5% sodium carbonate—100 ml; 0.1% eosin in water—100 ml; absolute methyl alcohol—100 ml.

Buffer solution: This is prepared using 49.6 ml of anhydrous disodium hydrogen phosphate with 50.4 ml of anhydrous potassium hydrogen phosphate.

Procedure: One drop of blood is taken by a capillary puncture using the lancet. After sterilization with surgical spirit on a clean glass slide, the blood drop is smeared using the edge of another slide and is allowed to dry at room temperature. Such a slide is mounted on a staining tray and flooded with Leishmann's stain using a dropper. After 4 minutes, it is diluted with the buffer solution and kept for 1 to 2 minutes. Then the slide is washed over the tap water and dried at room temperature before mounting it on the stage of the microscope. Using the stage mover, the slide is checked for the staining condition and then used for counting.

Counting procedure: Oil immersion objective is highly prepared for differential leucocyte count. A drop of cedar wood oil or any other such oil is added on the slide.

General observations: The blood film prepared should not be too thick or too thin. If the cover of the spreader slide is cut off, the smear occupies the slide only in the middle portion, so that the edges can be examined easily. This is of high value when the leucocytes are more in number at the edges. The slide must be thoroughly examined to verify whether clotting occurs in the smear because such a smear cannot give good results. Also the blood cells must be sufficiently stained well for easy differentiation. It is also important to note that ruleaux formation of erythrocytes does not occur.

Types of Leucocytes: Leucocytes can be broadly categorized as agranular and granular.

Agranular includes the following sub-types

a. **Monocyte:** It is the largest blood cell in human. The nucleus is kidney shaped and twisted. The cytoplasm has a frosty appearance without the granules.

Size: 10 μ; Function: Phagocytosis increases chronic infection; Normal value: 200-600/c-mm of blood (2–6%).

b. **Large Lymphocyte:** These are leucocytes with spherical nucleus and a clear basophilic cytoplasm.

   Normal value: 5–10%.

c. **Small Lymphocyte:** The nucleus is spherical and deeply stained. It occupies the major part of the cell with a ridge of strong basophilic cytoplasm.

   Size: 8–10 μ; Function: It provides the antibody; Normal value: 20–30%.

Granular leucocytes include the following sub-types

d. **Neutrophil:** The nucleus is usually divided irregularly into 2–5 lobes, connected to each other by means of fine strands. The cytoplasm is jointly pinkish and also gets filled with uniform sized granules which are also pink in colour. The cell is spherical with a distinct nuclear membrane and nucleoli. Such neutrophils are chemotactic and phagocytic causing destruction of pathogens such as bacteria through phagocytosis.

   Size: 10 to 20 μ; Function: Phagocytosis; Life: 3 to 5 days; Normal value: 60–70%.

e. **Eosinophil:** The nucleus is bilobed giving the appearance of a spectacle. Otherwise it is horse-shoe shaped or dumpbell shaped. The granules in the cytoplasm are compact, and coarse gaining the eosin colour. Also the cell is spherical in shape.

   Size: 10 to 12 μ; Function: destruction and detoxification of toxins; Life: 8–12 days; Normal value: 1–6%.

f. **Basophil:** The lobulation of the nucleus is distinct but it stains more faintly whereas the granules in the cytoplasm are purplish or bluish black. They are also known as mast cells.

Size: 8 to 10 µ; Function: Mediates reaction related to hypersensitivity and nodular inflammatory response by releasing heparin and proteins.

Normal value: 1% or less.

Clinical significance: Differential count is vital for the diagnosis of a number of blood related disorders. Increased neutrophil count is seen in a condition like microbial infection, Osteomyelitis, chicken pox, and some metabolic disorders such as diabetic ketosis, acute gout and tissue damage such as burns and Acute Myocardial Infarction. Decreased level is seen in bone marrow depression, typhoid, Brucellosis, collagen, vascular disease and also in the deficiency of folic acid and vitamin B_{12}.

Regarding eosinophil, increased level is seen in allergic conditions, necrosis of solid tumour, ulcerative colitis, adrenocortical hypofunction and pernicious anaemia, decreased level is seen in shock, burns and Cushing's syndrome. Increased level in basophil is seen in chronic myelocytic leukemia, polycythemia, haemolytic anaemia and nephrosis. Whereas decreased level is seen in pregnancy and hyperthyroidism.

With reference to monocytes, increased level happens in tuberculosis, sub-acute bacterial endocarditis, rocky mountain spotted fever, rheumatoid arthritis, carcinoma and monocytic leukemia. With reference to lymphocytes, increased level takes place in brucellosis, syphilis, tuberculosis, hepatitis, measles, ulcerative colitis and lymphocytic leukemia. Decreased level is noted in congestive heart failure, renal failure and immune suppression.

1.7 Reticulocyte Count

Aim: To determine reticulocyte count of blood smear.

Materials required: Cotton, spirit, lancet, glass slide, reticulocyte diluting fluid and microscope.

Principle: Reticulocytes are immature erythrocytes. They contain remnants of ribosomes and RNA which are present in large amount in the cytoplasm of nucleated precursor (Normoblast) from which they are derived. Ribosomes and

RNA react with certain dyes such as brilliant cresyl blue and form a precipitate of granules or filaments.

Composition of diluting fluid:

Brilliant cresyl blue	: 1.8 gm
Sodium citrate	: 0.48 gm
0.85 sodium chloride solution	: 100 ml

Procedure: A small amount of Brilliant cresyl blue is filtered and two drops are transferred into small test tubes. Two drops of blood are added and mixed. The test tube is then left undisturbed for 15 minutes at room temperature. After 15 minutes, the content of the tube is mixed well and a small drop of the mixture is removed and placed on a clean glass slide. A thin smear is prepared and allowed to air-dry to examine it under oil immersion objective.

Calculation:

$$\text{Reticulocyte count} = \frac{\text{Total reticulocytes count}}{\text{Number of RBC count}} \times 100$$

Normal value: Adults: 0.2–2%; Infants: 2–6%.

Clinical significance: The number of reticulocytes in the blood circulation indicates the degree of activity of bone marrow. If the bone marrow is very active, the number of reticulocytes increases. This is known as reticulocytosis. Reticulocytes decrease in aplastic anaemia which indicates the low activity of bone marrow. It increases in haemolytic anaemia.

1.8 Total Platelet Count

Aim: To find out the total platelet count of a person.

Material required: Haemocytometer, Sahli's pipette, cotton, surgical spirit, syringe with needle, serum tube, platelet diluting fluid, cover slip and microscope.

Principle: Platelets are the smallest cells in blood circulation. They precipitate in the blood clotting process. They originate from megakaryotes in the bone marrow. There are three different methods for platelet count namely haemocytometer method, blood smear method and automation method.

Counting procedure: Haemocytometry is a widely practiced method in which the diluent prevents coagulation due to citrate, fixes the platelets due to formalin and prevents them from clumping. However red cells are not lysed. Platelets are identified by shape, size and dark colour. Brilliant cresyl blue dye present in the diluent provides the background during cell counting but this does not stain the platelets and is not essential for the counting procedure.

Composition of diluting fluid:

1. Tri-sodium citrate (0.0106M) : 3.8 gm
2. 40% formaldehyde : 0.2 ml
3. Distilled water : 100 ml
4. Brilliant cresyl blue : 0.1 gm

Procedure: After cold sterilization using surgical spirit and cotton, blood is drawn with a syringe which is emptied in a serum tube that contains EDTA. 20 µl of such anticoagulated blood is drawn with the help of Sahli's pipette. It is then transferred into a test tube containing freshly filtered 3.98 ml of diluting fluid. The blood specimen and the diluent should be mixed well for at least 5 minutes. Using the Sahli's pipette, a drop of diluted specimen is loaded into the haemocytometer and kept undisturbed for 15 minutes. It is then mounted onto the stage of the compound light microscope. The left side counting area has to be focused under low power magnification. The platelets appear bluish and must be distinguished from debris. Platelets are oval, round or coma shaped refractile bodies that should be counted in the central ruled area (1 sq mm, i.e. all 25 small squares) of the Neubaur chamber.

Normal value: 3×10^5 platelets/µl of blood.

Clinical significance: Increased platelet count known as Thrombocytosis is found in certain clinical disorders such as polycythemia and chronic myogenesis leukemia, following splenectomy and other clinical conditions. Decreased platelet count known as thrombocytopenia occurs in certain other clinical disorders such as acute leukemia, aplastic anaemia, immune thrombocytopenia, megaloblastic anaemia, hypersplenism, following cytotoxic chemotherapy and radiation treatment. Enumeration of platelets is requested in the investigation of bleeding disorders such as Dengue Haemorrhagic fever. However, during enumeration, one should remember that platelets are very small cells and can easily float away and hence they should be allowed to settle down before counting. However, there are some possible errors. Platelet count must be done within two hours, and any delay causes disintegration of particles. Dust particles and debris are the most important sources of the errors, because they are easily mistaken for platelets. Hence glasswares should be kept clean. The diluting fluid has to be filtered before use. Still an error of 15–25% is frequently observed in platelet count.

1.9 Absolute Eosinophil Count

Aim: To determine the total eosinophil count.

Materials required: Sahli's pipette, lancet, cotton, spirit, haemocytometer, Dunger's fluid and microscope.

Composition of reagent:

Dunger's fluid

Eosin solution : 1%

CH_3-Co-CH_3 : 5 ml

Distilled water : 95 ml

50 gm of Eosin powder is dissolved in 95 ml of distilled water and 5 ml of acetone is added and then mixed well.

Principle: Blood is diluted with Dunger's fluid, which disintegrates the red cell and stains the eosinophil cell red. The diluted blood specimen is then loaded in a counting chamber. The cells are counted under high power in a known volume of fluid. Hence the count should not be delayed beyond 15–30 minutes after diluting the blood.

Procedure: 20 μl of anticoagulated blood is taken in a serum tube to which 0.38 ml of diluting fluid is added. Care must be taken to wipe the pipette before transferring the blood specimen to avoid false high values. The content of the pipette has to be washed at least three times with the diluting fluid taken in the serum tube.

The diluting fluid and blood specimen have to be mixed thoroughly and should be left for a few minutes without disturbance. Then the mixture is loaded in the Neubaur chamber and focused under the microscope. In case of routine white blood cell count, only the 4 corners of the ruled area have to be counted. The entire ruled area can be chosen for counting if the value in the 4 corners is one or less. However, it has to be done in correlation with the value of eosinophil in differential leucocyte count.

Normal value

Eosinophil/µl : 40–440/µl

Eosinophil (%) : 1–6% of differential leukocyte count.

Clinical significance: It gives the total number of eosinophils in the leucocyte population. Eosinophil has a close relationship with the adrenal function (e.g., Cushing's disease or hyperadrenalism is reflected by a full in eosinophil count. In fact, eosinophil count is requested as a part of adrenal function test. Increased eosinophil count is often associated with parasitic infection, allergic reaction, brucellosis, certain leukemia. It also increases during asthma, Hay fever, serum sickness, angiocurotic oedema, eczema, Hodgkin's disease, metastasis and necrosis of solid tumour.

REFERENCES

Assendelft, Van W., R.M. Rowan, F.E. Preston, 2002. *Advances Laboratory Methods in Haematology*, Oxford University.

Barbara, J. Bain, 1998. *Haematology*, Elsevier science health science division.

Barnard, D.L., B.A. Mc Verry, D.R. Morfolk, 1990. *Clinical Haematology*, Elsevier science health science division.

Brenner, K., 1996. *Recent Advances in Haematology*. Harcourt health sciences.

Chanarin, I., 1989. *Laboratory Haematology: An Account of Laboratory Techniques*, Elsevier science health science division.

Christopher, A. Ludlam, 1990. *Clinical Haematology*, Elsevier science health science division.

Drew, Provan, John Lilleyman, Andrew Provan, Charles R.J. Singer, Trevor Baglin, 2004. *Oxford Handbook of Clinical Haematology.*

Hoffbrond, A.V., J.E. Petit, 1987. *Clinical Haematology Illustrated—An Integrated Text and Color Atlas*, Churchill Livingstone.

Lawrence, T. Diamond, Doyen T. Nguyen, Lawrence W. Diamond, 2000. *Diagnostic Haematology: A Pattern Approach.*

2

Serology

Serum is the liquid part of the blood, normally a golden yellow colour that is left when the blood cells are removed. It is comprised of water (naturally) as well as a very high content of various proteins. These include albumin (protein that aids in the proper retention of water in the bloodstream), globulins (antibodies) and other useful proteins.

Serology is the scientific study of blood serum. In practice, the term usually refers to the *diagnostic* identification of antibodies in the serum. Such antibodies are typically formed in response to an infection (against a given *microorganism*), against other foreign proteins (in response, for example, to a mismatched *blood transfusion*), or to one's own proteins (in instances of *autoimmune disease*).

Serological tests may be performed for diagnostic purposes when an *infection* is suspected, in rheumatic illnesses, and in many other situations, such as checking an individual's *blood type*. Serology blood tests help to diagnose patients with certain immune deficiencies associated with the lack of *antibodies*, such as *X-linked gammaglobulinemia*. In such cases, tests for antibodies will be consistently negative.

There are several serology techniques that can be used depending on the antibodies being studied. These include *agglutination*, *precipitation*, *complement-fixation* and *fluorescent antibodies*. Some serological tests are not limited to blood serum, but can also be performed on other body fluids such as *semen* and *saliva*, which have (roughly) similar properties to serum. Serological tests may also be used *forensically*, generally to link a perpetrator to a piece of evidence (e.g., linking a rapist to a semen sample). Some important serological tests are given below.

2.1 Widal Test

(Widely Investigated Disease of Alimentary tract)

Aim: To detect the presence of antibodies against the bacteria *Salmonella typhi* and *Salmonella paratyphi.*

Materials required: Kit containing *Salmonella* antigens (O, H, AH, BH), positive control, negative control, droppers, applicator stick and ceramic slide.

Sample: Serum.

Separation of serum: Collect 5 ml of blood by venous puncture by using sterile dry syringe. Allow the blood to clot and the serum is separated. It should be free from haemolysis.

Principle: It is based on the principle of direct agglutination. When the patient's serum containing antibodies to *Salmonella typhi* and *Salmonella paratyphi* is mixed with the respective antigens, visible agglutination indicates the presence of antibodies to the particular antigen (O, H, AH, BH). A rising titre of antibody is indicative of enteric fever.

Procedure

I. Qualitative method (Screening slide test)

1. Place one drop of undiluted test serum in each of the first four circles and add 1 drop of positive control and negative control normal saline in each of the two circles respectively.
2. Add one drop of each antigen O, H, AH and BH in the first four circles and one drop of any one antigen in remaining two circles.
3. Mix the contents of each circle with separate applicator stick and spread well.
4. Rock the slide for two minutes and observe for agglutination.

Interpretation

- The absence of agglutination in the serum sample up to 2 minutes is negative reaction.
- If agglutination appears in any one of the first four circles, one has to do quantitative test to determine the antibody titre value.

II. Quantitative method (Confirmatory test)

1. If positive result is with any antigen, dilution of 1:20, 1:40, 1:80, 1:160, 1:320, 1:640, ..., etc. is made with the sample to be tested with normal saline (0.9%).

Preparation of Dilution

1. 1.1 ml of serum is mixed with 1.9 ml of normal saline for 1:20 dilution.
2. From this mixture 1 ml of diluted sample is drawn into another test tube to which add 1 ml (equal volume) of normal saline to get 1:40 dilution.
3. Likewise, dilute the serum sample up to 1:1280 (required/or more) to determine the antibody titre value.
4. Place one drop of diluted test serum in each circle (seven circles for 1:1280).
5. Add one drop of appropriate antigen suspension, which showed agglutination in the screening test.
6. Mix the contents with separate applicator stick.
7. Rock the slide gently for two minutes and examine for disappearance of agglutination.

Interpretation

- Agglutination test is carried out for each dilution till agglutination disappears.
- Agglutination titre value of 1:80 or more is significant.

Clinical significance: This test is mainly done for detection and diagnosis of enteric fever. The enteric fever includes typhoid and paratyphoid. Diseases caused by the bacilli,

Salmonella typhi and *Salmonella paratyphi*. *Salmonella typhi* and *Salmonella paratyphi* based on their antigenic structure are classified as 'O' (somatic) and 'H' (flagellar) antigens. 'O' antigens of various species have many common antigenic components. Hence, only one antigen — *Salmonella typhi* 'O' is used in the routine test. 'H' antigen is species specific. Therefore, 'H' antigens of *Salmonella typhi*, *Salmonella paratyphi* 'AH' and 'BH', which are commonly encountered in tropical countries, are used in the test. In enteric fever, specific agglutinins are usually detectable in patient blood after 6 days of fever. A rising titre at interval of 5-6 days is considered as diagnostically more significant than a single test result. Person immunized with TAB vaccine may show moderately high titre with all the antigens. Rise in 'O' titre alone results from anamnestic reaction.

2.2 Rapid Plasma Reagin (RPR) Test

(Test for Syphilis)

Aim: To detect the presence of reagin protein by the use of antigen for the diagnosis of Syphilis.

Materials required: RPR antigen, positive control, negative control, plastic white card, plastic droppers and applicator stick.

Sample: Serum.

Separation of serum: Collect 5 ml of blood by venous puncture by using sterile dry syringe. Allow the blood to clot and the serum is separated. It should be free from haemolysis.

Principle: Rapid plasma reagin antigen suspension is a carbon containing cardiolipin antigen, which detects reagin antibody present in serum of syphilis individuals. In addition it contains a balanced quantity of cholesterol and lecithin. Reagin is occasionally present in serum of person with acute or chronic conditions. When a specimen contains antibody flocculation occurs due to co-agglutination of carbon particles of RPR antigen, which appears as black clumps against the white background of the card.

Procedure

I. Qualitative method (Screening slide test)

1. Place one drop of serum in first circle, positive control in second circle and negative control in third circle.
2. Add one drop of well-mixed RPR antigen in three circles by using dropper.
3. Mix well and spread out the pool of liquid uniformly within the entire area of the circle by using applicator stick.
4. Rock the card gently to and fro for eight minutes either manually or on mechanical rotator at 100 rpm.
5. Read the results under good light source for the appearance of floccules.

Interpretation

- Appearance of strong black colour clumps within eight minutes is positive reaction. It indicates presence of reagin antibodies.
- Absence of black aggregates at the end of eight minutes is negative reaction.

II. Quantitative method

1. If positive reaction, dilute the serum sample serially with normal saline from 1:2, 1:4, 1:8, 1:16, 1:32... 1:1024.

Preparation of Dilution

I. To 0.1 ml of serum add equal volume (0.1 ml) of saline and mixed to get 1:1 dilution.

II. From this mixture 0.1 ml is drawn into another test tube and add 0.1 ml of normal saline to get 1:2 dilution.

III. And further dilutions are made, such as 1:4, 1:8......1:1024 (required/or more) and from final dilution 0.1 ml is discarded.

2. Place one drop of each diluted serum sample in circle of the disposable plastic test card.

3. Add one drop of well-mixed RPR antigen in all circles by using dropper.
4. Mix well and spread out the pool of liquid uniformly within the entire area of the circle by using applicator stick.
5. Rock the card gently to and fro for eight minutes either manually or on mechanical rotator at 100 rpm.
6. Read the results under good light source for the appearance of floccules.

Interpretation Prorated

- To observe the end point in the highest dilution showing any visible aggregation of black particle.

Clinical significance: Syphilis is a sexually transmitted disease (STD) and caused by the organism *Treponema pallidum* by direct contact but some time indirect contact. It has the power of gaining entrance to the body through minute lesions of the skin or mucous membrane.

Infection is usually rendered evident by the development of a primary lesion or chancre which appears within a month of infection and is accompanied by enlargement of the local lymph nodes from 6-12 weeks after the appearance of primary chancre, the secondary stage of the disease sets in; which shows symptoms like cutaneous lesion enlargement of lymph nodes and affects bones, joints, eyes and other organs. Then it becomes latent and can only be detected by serological test. This may persist for many years or till the patient's lifetime. In minority of patients late lesions appear. These may be benign, vecerating lesions of the skin, mucous membrane bones or gummate of the internal organs. More serious are lesions of the heart, producing aneurysms or of the nervous system of which Tabes dorsalis and general paralysis are the most common. To confirm the diagnosis, the test should be reactive in 1/16 dilution or more.

2.3 Detection of Rheumatoid Factor

Aim: To detect rheumatoid factor by latex agglutination test.

Materials required: Latex gamma globulin reagent, positive control, negative control, slide, droppers and applicator stick.

Sample: Serum.

Separation of serum: Collect 5 ml of blood by venous puncture by using sterile dry syringe. Allow the blood to clot and the serum is separated. It should be free from haemolysis.

Principle: The Rheumatoid factor latex reagent is a suspension of polystyrene latex particles of uniform size, coated with human gamma globulin. When a serum sample positive for rheumatoid factor is mixed with latex reagent, visible agglutination occurs. In samples negative for rheumatoid factor, the latex remains in a smooth suspension form. The sensitivity of the latex reagent is 20 IU/ml or more of the rheumatoid factor will show a clear agglutination.

Procedure

I. Qualitative method

1. Place one drop of test serum within the circled area and marked as test.
2. Add one drop of latex gamma globulin reagent to the serum and mix well with a disposable applicator stick.
3. For positive and negative control follow the same procedure as in the test.
4. Rock the slide gently to and fro for two minutes and examine for agglutination. Do not examine beyond two minutes.

Interpretation

- Agglutination visible within two minutes is to be interpreted as positive reaction.
- No agglutination is to be considered as negative reaction.
- Sensitivity of the test is 20 IU/ml. (It may vary depending on the manufacturers.)
- The following conclusion may be drawn depending upon the observations as follows:

Observation	Conclusion
Coarse agglutination (agglutination occur within one minute) positive	Strongly
Fine agglutination (agglutination occur within two minutes) positive	Weakly
Smooth suspension (without any major change)	Negative

II. Quantitative method

1. If positive reaction, dilute the serum sample serially with normal saline from 1:2, 1:4, 1:8, 1:16, 1:32... 1:1024.

Preparation of dilution

I. To 0.1 ml of serum add equal volume (0.1 ml) of saline and mixed to get 1:1 dilution.

II. From this mixture 0.1 ml is drawn into another test tube and add 0.1 ml of normal saline to get 1:2 dilution.

III. And further dilutions are made, such as 1:4, 1:8... 1:1024 (required/or more) and from final dilution 0.1 ml is discarded.

2. Place one drop of diluted serum sample using separate plastic droppers in each circle of slide.
3. Add one drop of latex gamma globulin reagent in each of the circle mix well with applicator stick.
4. Rock the slide gently back and forth for two minutes and observe for agglutination.

Interpretation

- Agglutination in the highest serum dilution corresponds to provide approximate amount of rheumatoid factor concentration present in the serum.
- Concentration of RF can be calculated by

  Rf in IU/ml = Sensitivity of the test × highest dilution of the serum showing agglutination.

Clinical significance: The Rheumatoid factor test is done in order to detect the presence of rheumatoid factors in the serum of the patients with rheumatoid arthritis. Higher titre of RF is usually related to the severity of rheumatoid arthritis. Rheumatoid factor may be present in low concentrations in 3-5 per cent of the normal population. This percentage increases with the age of population. This factor is non-specific. Positive results may occur occasionally in various pathological disease states including systemic lupus erythematosus, hepatitis, cirrohosis, lymphomas, hypergamaglobulinemia, scleroderma and sarcoidosis. Quantitative analysis helps to monitor the therapy of Rheumatoid Arthritis.

2.4 C-Reactive Protein (CRP) Test

Aim: To determine the titre of C-reactive protein in serum.

Materials required: CRP latex reagent, positive control, negative control, slide, drop pers and applicator stick.

Sample: Serum.

Separation of serum: Collect 5 ml of blood by venous puncture by using sterile dry syringe. Allow the blood to clot and the serum is separated. It should be free from haemolysis.

Principle: C-reactive protein latex slide test is used for the detection of C-reaction protein and is based on the principle of agglutination. The test specimen is mixed with CRP reagent and allowed to react. If CRP concentrations are greater than 0.6 mg/100 ml a visible agglutination is observed and if less than 0.6 mg then no agglutination is observed.

Procedure

I. Qualitative method

1. One drop of the test serum is placed on the slide using a disposable dropper.
2. Add one drop of CRP latex reagent to test specimen on the slide.
3. Mix the test specimen and latex reagent uniformly over the entire circle with the help of applicator stick.
4. Rock the slide gently, back and forth, and observe agglutination macroscopically within two minutes.

Interpretation

- Presence of agglutination indicates positive reaction.
- Presence of detectable level of CRP in the test serum—above 0.6 mg/100 ml.
- Absence of agglutination indicates negative reaction.
- Absence of detectable level of CRP in the test serum—below 0.6 mg/100 ml.

II. Quantitative method

1. If positive reaction, the test serum is diluted serially in the ratio of 1:2, 1:4, 1:8, 1:16...1:1024 by using normal saline.

Preparation of Dilution

I. To 0.1 ml of serum add equal volume (0.1 ml) of saline and mixed to get 1:1 dilution.

II. From this mixture 0.1 ml is drawn into another test tube and add 0.1 ml of normal saline to get 1:2 dilution.

III. And further dilutions are made, such as 1:4, 1:8... 1:1024 (required/or more) and from final dilution 0.1 ml is discarded.

2. Place one drop of diluted serum sample using separate plastic droppers in each circle of slide.
3. To each of the circle one drop of C-reactive protein latex reagent is added and mixed well with the help of applicator stick.
4. Mix the test specimen and latex reagent uniformly over the entire circle with the help of applicator stick.
5. Rock the slide gently, back and forth, and observe agglutination macroscopically within two minutes.

Interpretation

- Agglutination in the highest serum dilution corresponds to provide approximate amount of C-reactive protein concentration present in the serum.
- Concentration of the C-reactive protein can be calculated as follows:

CRP in mg/100 ml = Sensitivity of the test × Highest dilution of the serum showing agglutination.

Clinical significance: CRP is serum protein, which is synthesized in the liver and this test is non-specific. CRP is found in low concentration in the serum of healthy individual. The increase in CRP level is generally associated with many conditions like rheumatic diseases, pregnancy, use of oral contraceptives, etc. The C-reactive protein test can also help in determining post-surgical complications. Its use in the post-operative surveillance is of great importance. CRP levels invariably rise after major surgery but fall to normal within 7-10 days. Absence of this fall is indicative of possible septic or inflammatory post-operative complications. Raised high sensitive CRP levels are seen during Acute Coronary syndrome. It is lowered with statin therapy.

2.5 Anti-Streptolysin 'O' (ASO) Test

Aim: To estimate the level of anti-streptolysin O antibodies by slide agglutination method.

Materials required: ASO latex antigen, positive control, negative control, droppers, disposable plastic slide and applicator stick.

Sample: Serum.

Separation of serum: Collect 5 ml of blood by venous puncture by using sterile dry syringe. Allow the blood to clot and the serum is separated. It should be free from haemolysis.

Principle: The anti-streptolysin O latex test contains polysterene latex particles coated with purified and stabilized streptolysin O (antigen) which reacts with its corresponding anti-streptolysin O (antibody) in the test sample, resulting in the agglutination of latex particles.

Procedure

I. Qualitative method

1. Using disposable plastic dropper, place one drop of serum in circled area of the slide provided in the kit.

2. Add one drop of anti-streptolysin O latex antigen to serum and mix well with applicator stick.
3. For positive and negative controls follow the same procedure as in the test.
4. Rock the slide gently to and fro and examine for agglutination within two minutes.

Interpretation

- Appearance of agglutination indicates positive reaction, which indicates presence of detectable amount of antibody (ASO) in serum (above 200 IU/ml).
- Absence of agglutination indicates negative reaction (below 200 IU/ml).

II. Quantitative method

1. If positive reaction, the test serum is diluted serially in the ratio of 1:2, 1:4, 1:8, 1:16...1:1024 by using normal saline.

Preparation of Dilution

I. To 0.1 ml of serum add equal volume (0.1 ml) of saline and mixed to get 1:1 dilution.

II. From this mixture 0.1 ml is drawn into another test tube and add 0.1 ml of normal saline to get 1:2 dilution.

III. And further dilutions are made, such as 1:4, 1:8... 1:1024 (required/or more) and from final dilution 0.1 ml is discarded.

2. Place one drop of diluted serum sample using separate plastic droppers in each circles of slide.
3. To each of the circle one drop of ASO latex reagent is added and mixed well with the help of applicator stick.
4. Mix the test specimen and latex reagent uniformly over the entire circle with the help of applicator stick.
5. Rock the slide gently, back and forth, and observe agglutination macroscopically within two minutes.

Interpretation

- Agglutination in the highest serum dilution corresponds to provide approximate amount of ASO concentration present in the serum.
- Concentration of the ASO can be calculated as follows:

ASO IU/ml = Sensitivity of the test × Highest dilution of the serum showing agglutination.

Clinical significance: The ASO test is still more popular test used in the diagnosis and monitoring of streptococcal infections and rheumatic fever. Increased ASO titre is associated with acute streptococcal infection (*Streptococcus pyogenes*), rheumatic fever, and glomerulonephritis. The titre of ASO should be observed repeatedly over a time of 4 to 6 weeks in case of suspected streptococcal infection. *S. pyogenes* produces a number of toxins; the two of significance here are streptolysin O (SL) and hyaluronidase. The patient following streptococcal infection produces the corresponding antibodies. The diagnosis of a sore throat due to *S. pyogenes* infection is done by the culture of a throat swab specimen. Mere positive ASO titre does not confirm Acute Rheumatic Fever. Modified Jone's criteria must be used.

2.6 Detection of Hepatitis B Surface Antigen (HBsAg)

Aim: To detect Hepatitis B surface antigen by one step card (slide) test method.

Materials required: Herp-Alert B.

Sample: Serum.

Separation of serum: Collect 5 ml of blood by venous puncture by using sterile dry syringe. Allow the blood to clot and the serum is separated. It should be free from haemolysis.

Principle: This test uses solid phase immunochromatographic technology for the qualitative detection of HBsAg in serum or plasma. The test is a two-site immunometric assay in which a combination of monoclonal and polyclonal antibodies are used to selectively detect HBsAg in serum with a high degree of sensitivity. Each device has a Reading window with an upper 'control' region and the lower 'test' region and a sample well. In the test procedure, 2-3 drops of serum sample is added to the well and allowed to soak in. Read result within 20 minutes. If HBsAg is present in the specimen, it will react with the conjugate dye, which binds to the antibody on the membrane to generate a coloured line. Presence of two coloured lines, one in the test zone and other in the control zone, indicates a positive result, while the absence of the line in the test zone indicates a negative result.

Procedure

1. Remove the testing device from the foil pouch by tearing at the 'notch' and place on a leveled surface.
2. Holding the sample dropper vertically, add 2-3 drops of the specimen into the sample well-marked 'S'.
3. Read results within 20 minutes.

Interpretation

- **Positive:** Red purple bands appearing in the test (t) and the control (c) zones, indicate the presence of HBsAg in the specimen.
- **Negative:** One red-purple band appearing in the control zone (c) with no band in the test zone (t) indicates that there is no HBsAg in the specimen or the concentration of HBsAg in the specimen is below the detectable level.
- **Invalid:** There is no colour band visible in the test zone and in the control zone or there is a visible band only in the test zone and not in the control zone. The test is considered to be invalid either due to deterioration of the test or an improper testing procedure.

Sensitivity: One step card test can be detected HBsAg in a sample at a concentration 0.40 unit/ml.

Clinical significance: One step immunochromatographic test is, for the detection of Hepatitis B surface Antigen in human serum. Viral hepatitis is a systematic disease primarily involving the liver. Most cases of acute viral hepatitis are due to A and B virus, or C virus. Hepatitis B virus was discovered by Blumberg, *et al.* A complex antigen found on the surface of HBV is called HBsAg. The presence of HBsAg in a serum sample is indicative of a HBV infection, either acute or chronic. In a typical HBV infection, HBsAg becomes detectable 2-4 weeks after the development of symptoms.

2.7 Detection of ABO Blood Grouping and Rh Typing

Aim: To detect ABO grouping and Rh typing of human blood sample.

Materials required: Antisera A, B & D, lancet, cotton, rectified spirit and porcelain tile.

Method: Slide method and Tube method.

Sample: Blood collected with or without anticoagulant may be used.

Principle: Blood grouping for A, B, O and Rh typing are the first steps of laboratory procedure before proceeding for cross matching the blood of recipient with that of donor. Human red blood cells possess A, B, or AB antigen on their cell surface. This antigen will agglutinate the corresponding antibodies, which are present in the antisera used. Human red blood cell possessing the Rh (D) antigen, which will agglutinate the anti D and give the appearance of clump on the slide. No clump on the slide indicates negative reaction.

Appearance of agglutination	= Respective blood group (A/B/or AB)
Blood group O	= No agglutination
Appearance of agglutination	= Rh Positive
No agglutination	= Rh Negative

Procedure

I. Rapid slide method

1. A porcelain tile is taken and divided into 3 parts with the help of wax pencil and marked as A, B and D (Rh).
2. Place one drop of reagent antisera A, B and D on porcelain tile.
3. To each reagent drop, add one drop of whole blood.

4. Mix well with an applicator stick uniformly and spread as a circle.
5. Rock the porcelain tile back and forth to complete the mixing.
6. Observe the agglutination reaction macroscopically within two minutes.
7. Same procedure can be adopted with antisera A1 and A2, if the individual belongs to A or AB group.

II. Modified tube method

1. Prepare 2-4% suspension of RBCs in saline.
2. Take 3 small test tubes and add one drop of anti A, anti B, anti D in each tube.
3. Add one drop of cell suspension to these 3 test tubes and mix well.
4. Allow standing for five minutes at room temperature and centrifuge for 1000 rpm for one minute or allowing the tubes to stand at room temperature for one hour.
5. Observe the tubes for microscopic or macroscopic agglutination.

Interpretation of results

- Agglutination with anti A – A group
- Agglutination with anti B – B group
- Agglutination in both anti A & B – AB group
- No agglutination in both anti A & B – O group
- Agglutination with anti D – Rh positive
- No agglutination with anti D – Rh negative

Clinical significance: The human blood group is often defined in accordance with the presence or absence of one or the other or both of the antigens known as A or B, on the surface of red blood cell. Next to the ABO system the major blood group is Rh system. In human beings of most races, 85 per cent possess the Rh antigen (Rhesus factor on their blood cell). The classification of human blood group is very much important when transfusion of blood from one person to the other person is to carry out. The incompatible transfusion may lead to serious anaphylactic reaction.

The slide method procedure alone is not reliable unless it is confirmed by tube method and the cross matching technique before the blood is transfused. It is mandatory that every individual needs to know his or her blood grouping and Rh typing. Since it is of great importance for the following conditions:

i. Transfusion of blood is of utmost importance in traumatic conditions or when the blood volume decreases either due to disorders or diseases.

ii. Detection of blood grouping and Rh typing helps in medicolegal parental dispute of an individual because the synthesis of antigens A, B and Rh are under the expression of genes from birth.

iii. In cases of rape and criminal conditions such as murder, DNA sequencing procedure can be adopted to identify the culprit.

2.8 Detection of Pregnancy

Aim: To detect human chorionic gonadotropin (hCG) by one step pregnancy card (slide) test method.

Materials required: Rapicheck hCG test device.

Sample: Urine.

Specimen collection and storage

1. For optimal detection of early pregnancy, a first morning specimen is preferred since it contains the higher concentration of hCG. However, randomly collected urine specimens may be used.
2. Collect a urine specimen in a clean glass or plastic container. Do not use preservatives.
3. If the test is not to be run immediately following sample collection, the sample can be stored for 48 hours at 2-8°C. Bring the specimen before testing.

4. If longer storage of the specimen is required, the specimen should be frozen (–20°C or below).
5. A frozen specimen should not be used if stored for more than two weeks. Prior to testing, the frozen specimen must be completely thawed, thoroughly mixed and brought to room temperature.

Principle: The immunochromatographic card contains a unique set of dye-conjugated and immobilized antibodies to hCG used to produced a distinctive visual pattern indicating elevated levels of hCG (> 25 IU/ml) in the test sample. In the test procedure, the urine sample is allowed to migrate through the absorbent area. If the sample contains detectable levels of hCG, the labeled antibody-dye conjugate binds to it, forming an antibody-antigen complex. As the reaction mixture continues to flow along the test membrane, the complex binds to the anti-hCG antibody coated in the test (t) zone and produces a dark red-purple colour band. The unbound conjugate binds to the reagents immobilized in the control (c) zone producing a dark red-purple colour band, demonstrating a valid test performance.

Procedure

1. Remove the testing device from the foil pouch by tearing at the 'notch' and place it on a leveled surface.
2. Holding the sample dropper vertically, add three drops of the urine specimen into the sample well marked 's'.
3. Read results after five minutes.

Interpretation

- **Positive (pregnancy):** Red-purple bands appearing in the test (t) and the control (c) regions, indicate the presence of > 25 IU/ml hCG in the specimen.
- **Negative:** One red-purple band appearing in the control region with no band in the test region, indicates that the concentration of hCG in the sample is below the detectable level.
- **Invalid:** There is no colour band visible both in the test region and in the control region or there is a visible

band only in the test region and not in the control region. The result is considered to be invalid either due to deterioration of the test or an improper testing procedure.

Clinical significance: Human chorionic gonadotropin (hCG) is a glycopeptide hormone produced by the placenta during pregnancy. The early appearance and rapid rise in the levels of hCG during pregnancy make it a good marker for pregnancy. Usually, concentration of hCG in urine reaches approximately 25 IU/ml as early as seven to ten days after conception. The concentration increases steadily and reaches its maximum between the 8th and 12th week of pregnancy. The Rapicheck hCG test is an immunochromatographic assay which utilizes monoclonal antibodies to hCG.

REFERENCES

Ryan, K.J. and Ray, C.G., 2004. *Sherris Medical Microbiology*, 4th Ed., McGraw Hill, 247-49.

Washington, J.A., 1996. "Principles of Diagnosis: Serodiagnosis" in *Baron's Medical Microbiology* (Baron, S. *et al.* eds.), 4th Ed., University of Texas Medical Branch.

3

Blood Bank Analysis

Blood bank stores and processes blood or blood plasma received from donors. It is then issued to recipients in need, as and when required. Blood bank consists of two units. One is collection of blood and its storage and the other unit is issuing of blood to recipients. Blood banks should participate in internal and external quality control proficiency testing program.

Human body contains 5–6 liters of blood and 300 cc of blood' can be withdrawn at one time. This volume is replenished in 48–72 hours and hemoglobin level in 4–5 weeks time. The amount of blood that is allowed to donate can be calculated by:

$$\frac{\text{Donor's weight}}{110} \times 450 = \text{Amount in ml allowed to donate.}$$

3.1 Blood Donors

Blood donors are the main source of blood and its components. There are three types of donors:

1. Voluntary donor—Donates the blood of his own free will. He does not accept any incentive or reward from the collecting agency.
2. Replacement donor—A member of the family or friend of the patient donates blood in replacement of the needed blood of the particular patient without any expectation of benefit.

3. Paid donor—Professional blood donors donate blood for direct or indirect benefits.

3.2 Donor Selection Criteria

Sl. No.	Criteria	Required condition
1	Age	Between 18-55 years
2	Body weight	49.5 Kg for donating 450 ml blood
3	Oral temperature	Not exceeding 37.5°C
4	Pregnancy	Pregnant woman cannot donate blood
5	Interval between blood donation	12 weeks
6	Pulse	72 per minute
7	Blood pressure	Systolic: 125 mm/Hg Diastolic: 75 mm/Hg
8	Hemoglobin	Male: More than 13.5 gm/dl Female: More than 12.5 gm/dl
9	Haematocrit	Male: More than 41% Female: More than 38%
10	Time of collection	At least 3 hours after meal
11	Chronic diseases	Should not be suffering from any chronic diseases
12	Vaccination	Cannot donate blood up to 3 weeks
13	Transmissible diseases through blood transfusion	
	a) AIDS	Negative
	b) Viral hepatitis	Negative
	c) Cytomegalovirus	Negative
	d) Malaria	Negative
	e) Filariasis	Negative
	f) American trypanosomiasis	Negative
	g) African trypanosomiasis	Negative
	h) Kala azar	Negative
	i) Syphilis and Yaws	Negative

3.3 Blood Collection

1. The room used to collect blood should be well ventilated with pleasant surroundings. Best site of puncture is checked first such as upper arm, which is an ideal site. Palpate for visible vein.
2. Keep the site as sterile as possible with correct chemical for cleaning depending on the test. Antiseptic such as 70 per cent isopropyl alcohol can be used to prevent microbial contamination of patient and sample.
3. Clean the site using a circular motion starting at the center of the site and moving outward in concentric circles applying enough pressure to remove the surface dirt.
4. Apply a pressure cuff to the upper arm and inflate it between 80-100 mm/Hg to make the veins more prominent.
5. Insert the needle level up and in alignment to vein, blood flow and tape the needle in place. Insert the needle into the skin at about 15 to 30 degrees angle using a smooth motion penetrating the skin and vein. Try to feel or hear the popping sound as needle penetrates the vein.
6. Decrease the pressure of the cuff between 40-60 mm/Hg as soon as blood begins to flow. Ask the donor to squeeze a small rubber ball.
7. When the level of blood has reached the desired mark, bring the pressure to zero. Seal the tubing 4-5 inches from the needle with the help of metal clip.
8. Use clean surgical cotton and with firm moderate pressure on top of the puncture site, quickly and swiftly remove the needle maintaining the pressure. Ask the patient to maintain the pressure on site.
9. If bleeding continues after 5 minutes, raise the arm of the patient in the air above the heart level for approximately 3-5 minutes. Instruct the patient to leave the bandage on for at least 15 minutes.

3.4 Anticoagulants

Anticoagulants are substances, which interfere with blood coagulation and thus prolong the coagulation time. Anticoagulants are important in the blood collection procedure. Commonly used anticoagulants in blood banks are:

Acid citrate dextrose (ACD) solution:

Composition

Dextrose	:	2.45 gm
Tri-sodium citrate	:	2.20 gm
Citric acid	:	0.89 gm
Fresh distilled water	:	100 ml
pH	:	5.5
Ratio of anticoagulant volume to 100 ml of whole blood	:	1.5 ml

Solution is filtered through sintered glass filter funnel into a clean container. Then it is sterilized at 20 degree celsius for 30 minutes immediately after its preparation.

Citrate phosphate dextrose (CPD) solution:

Composition

Tri-sodium citrate	:	2.63 gm
Citric acid	:	0.327 gm
Dextrose	:	2.55 gm
Monobasic sodium phosphate	:	0.222 gm
Fresh distilled water	:	100 ml
Ratio of anticoagulant volume to 100 ml of whole blood	:	1.4 ml

Solution is filtered through sintered glass filter funnel into a clean container. Then it is sterilized at 20 degree celsius for 30 minutes immediately after its preparation. C.P.D. anticoagulants have a better post transfusion survival of red blood cells than other anticoagulants.

Heparin solution:

Heparin solution	:	7500 U
Fresh distilled water	:	100 ml

Blood collected in heparin solution must be used within 48 hours.

Citrate phosphate dextrose adenine (CPDA 1) solution:

Adenine maintains viability of red blood cells for 35 days.

Ethylene diamine tetra acetic acid (EDTA)

It is not used as anticoagulant in blood bank to collect blood because it has strong chelating agent.

3.5 Blood Derived Components

Sl.No.	Blood component	Storage time	Possible uses
1	Packed cells	4 hours-1 day	Anaemia's, kidney, liver and cardiovascular diseases.
2	Fresh frozen plasma (FFP)	21 days-few months	Dehydration, severe burns cases, protein deficiency, maintenance of blood volume and clotting factors deficiency.
3	Cryoprecipitate	1 year	Von Willebrand's disease, Haemophilia A, afibrinogenaemia.
4	Fibrinogen	5 years	Afibrinogenaemia and blood coagulation disease
5	Leucocytes	1 day	Agranulocytosis and granulocytopenia in certain leukemias.
6	Platelets	1 day	Platelet disorder, thrombocytopenia and leukaemic conditions and Dengue Haemorrhagic fever

3.6 Blood Group System

Blood group system plays main role in blood transfusion. There are nearly 300 blood groups systems. Only ABO blood group system and Rh system are considered important as they cause serious complications in blood transfusion. ABO blood group system was discovered by Karl Landsteiner in 1900. In 1937, Landsteiner and Wiener discovered new blood factor known as Rh.

Antigen and antibodies in ABO blood group system:

Blood Group	Red cell antigen	Antibody in serum
A	A	B
B	B	A
AB	Both A&B	None
O	None	Both A&B

3.6.1 ABO Grouping

Aim: To determine the ABO blood grouping of given test sample by slide and tube method.

Principle: A and B antigens present in human red cells agglutinates in the presence of antibody directed towards the antigen. Agglutination of red cells with respective anti A, anti B, anti AB reagents is a positive test result and indicates the presence of the corresponding antigen. Absence of agglutination of red cells with anti A, anti B, anti AB reagents is a negative test result and indicates the absence of the corresponding antigen.

Reagents required: ABO blood grouping kit, saline, standard glasswares.

Procedure

Slide ABO grouping

1. One drop of anti A, anti B, anti AB, reagents are placed in the corresponding circles on a clean slide.
2. To each drop of reagent, one drop of whole blood is added.
3. Mixed well and the slide is rocked back and forth gently. Agglutination is observed macroscopically at two minutes and microscopically under 45x objective.

Tube ABO grouping

1. 2-3 per cent red cell suspension is prepared and three clean test tubes are taken.
2. One drop of anti A, anti B, anti AB is placed in correspondingly labeled test tubes.

3. One drop of red cell suspension is added in each test tube and mixed well.
4. Tubes are centrifuged for 1-3 minutes at 1000 rpm or incubated at room temperature for 30 minutes.
5. After centrifugation, the cells are resuspended and agglutination is observed macroscopically.
6. One drop of resuspended cells are placed on the slide and observed microscopically under 45x objective for agglutination.

Results

Agglutination with anti A	:	A group
Agglutination with anti B	:	B group
Agglutination with anti A, anti B	:	AB group
No Agglutination with anti A, anti B	:	O group

3.6.2 RHESUS TYPING

Aim: To determine the Rh typing of given test sample by slide and tube method.

Principle: Rh antigen present in human red cells agglutinates in the presence of antibody directed towards the antigen. Agglutination of red cells with anti D (IgM) monoclonal reagent is a positive test result and indicates the presence of the corresponding antigen. Absence of agglutination of red cells with anti D (IgM) monoclonal reagent is a negative test result and indicates the absence of the corresponding antigen.

Reagents required: Anti D monoclonal reagent, saline, standard glasswares.

Procedure

Slide test

1. One drop of anti D (IgM) monoclonal reagent is placed on a clean slide.
2. To the drop of reagent, one drop of whole blood is added.

3. Mixed well and the slide is rocked back and forth gently. Agglutination is observed macroscopically at two minutes and microscopically under 45x objective.

Tube test

1. 2–3% red cell suspension is prepared and clean test tube is taken.
2. One drop of anti D (IgM) monoclonal reagent is placed in labeled test tube.
3. One drop of red cell suspension is added in test tube and mixed well.
4. Tubes are centrifuged for 1–3 minutes at 1000 rpm or incubated at room temperature for 30 minutes.
5. After centrifugation, the cells are resuspended and agglutination is observed macroscopically.
6. One drop of resuspended cells are placed on slide and observed microscopically under 45x objective for agglutination.

Results: Agglutination with anti D: Positive (+)
No agglutination with anti D: Negative (–).

3.7 Cross Matching

Aim: To determine the compatibility in donors blood to recipient blood.

Principle: Cells coated with an autoagglutinin or suspended in serum having protein abnormality may give a false positive result in Rh typing. Bovine albumin is frequently used as a control for Rh typing. Every blood sample tested by slide or modified tube method should be controlled by testing simultaneously with medium such as Bovine albumin.

Reagents required: Saline, anti human serum, coombs control cells, anti-D reagent, standard glasswares.

Major cross matching

Procedure: Major cross matching involves four phases:

Initial phase

1. Two small test tubes are labelled as S for saline and A for albumin.
2. Five per cent suspension of the donor's is red blood cells are prepared.
3. Two drops of recipient's serum is added to each test tube, one drop of donor's red cell is added to each test tube.
4. Two drops of Bovine albumin is added to the albumin labelled tube.
5. Both tubes are centrifuged for 15 seconds at 3500 rpm or 1 minute at 1000 rpm. After centrifugation, both tubes are examined macroscopically for haemolysis and agglutination.

Incubation phase

6. The saline tube is incubated at room temperature and the albumin tube at 37°C for 15 minutes. If desired, incubation may be extended up to 60 minutes.
7. Both tubes are centrifuged for 15 seconds at 3500 rpm or 1 minute at 1000 rpm. After centrifugation, both tubes are examined macroscopically for haemolysis and agglutination.

Antiglobulin phase

8. The cells in albumin tube are washed thoroughly with saline. Two drops of anti human serum is added to the washed cells, mixed and centrifuged for 15 seconds at 3500 rpm or 1 minute at 1000 rpm.
9. After centrifugation, the cells are resuspended and agglutination is observed both macroscopically and microscopically.
10. To all negative antiglobulin tubes, one drop of coombs control cells are added.

Preparation of Coombs control cells

11. Anti-D monoclonal antibodies for slide test and modified tube test is diluted (1:10) in saline.

12. Equal volume of this dilution is added to 10 per cent cell suspension of Group O Rh (D) positive red blood cells and incubated at 37°C for 30 minutes for sensitization.
13. After incubation, the cells are washed thrice with fresh saline and again 3-4 per cent sensitized cell suspension is prepared in saline.
14. One drop of these coombs control cell suspension is added to negative antiglobulin test.
15. After mixing, centrifuge for 15 seconds at 3500 rpm or 1 minute at 1000 rpm.
16. Examine macroscopically for haemolysis and agglutination.

Minor cross matching

The serum of the donor is tested against the red cell of the recipient. The procedure remains the same as for major cross matching.

Interpretation

1. Agglutination should not be visible in any phase.
2. Incompatibility in the saline phase should be investigated in the line of ABO grouping. Haemolysis indicates the presence of cold antibodies.
3. Haemagglutination at the anti human globulin phase detects antibodies such as anti-Fy (Duffy), anti-Jk (Kidd), etc.

REFERENCES

Eugene Braunwald, Anthony S. Fauci, Dennis L. Kasper, Stephen L. Hauser, Dan L. Longo, J. Larry Jameson, 2001. *Harrisons Principle of International Medicine*, Vol. 1, 15th edition, McGraw Hill Medical Publishing Division.

Geo F. Brooks, Janet S. Butel, Stephen A. Morse, Jawetz Melnick and Adelbergs, 2002. *Medical Microbiology*, 22nd edition, McGraw Hill Publications.

John Bernard Henry, 2001. *Clinical diagnosis and management by laboratory methods*, 20th edition, Saunders Company.

Kanai, L. Mukherjee, 2002. *Medical Laboratory Technology—A procedure manual for routine diagnostic tests*, Tata McGraw Hill Publishing, 11th edition.

Manual of Basic Techniques for a Health Laboratory, 2005. *World Health Orgainzation*, 2nd edition, New Age International.

Praful, B. Gofkar and Darshan P. Godkar, 2003. *Textbook of Medical Technology*, III edition, Bhalani Publications.

Ramnik Sood, 2002. *Medical Laboratory Technology—Methods and Interpretation*, Brother Publications, V edition.

4

Clinical Biochemistry

Studies in blood serum have gained much importance in recent years in the field of clinical biochemistry. In a clinical chemistry laboratory, we primarily deal with the analysis of the chemical constituents of various body fluids, the most important being the serum or plasma of all the routine analysis such as Haematology, Serology, Biochemistry and Fluid Analysis. Much attention has been paid to the biochemical analysis since it paves the way to arrive at the exact cause of a particular disease. We study clinical chemistry, since most of the analysis reflects on the biochemical malfunctioning of the vital organs such as liver, heart, kidney and brain, most of the biochemical analysis that is performed will lead to a coloured product and the intensity of the colour produced is directly proportional to the amount of that particular biochemical component of the body and can be read either by colorimetric or spectrometric methods in order to get the exact values. Clinical chemistry involves tests that can be primarily grouped into two basic types: 1. Non-enzymatic analysis, and 2. Test for enzymes.

Nonenzymatic Analysis

It includes Glucose, Urea, Uric acid, Creatinine, Cholesterol, Serum bilirubin and electrolytes such as Sodium, Potassium, Fluoride, Chloride and Bicarbonate.

Test for Enzymes

It includes Serum glutamate Oxalate Transaminase (AST), Serum glutamate Phosphate Transaminase (ALT), Acid phosphatase, Alkaline phosphatase, Gamma GT, LDH, Creatinine phosphokinase.

These make up the important enzymes in clinical chemistry. Enzymes are organic substances that accelerate a chemical reaction. The enzymes couple with the substrate to form enzyme substrate complex which in some cases breaks down to a product which may be coloured, while others do not. The product thus released is proportional to the enzymes concentration. Based on the enzyme activity four basic categories are recognized.

1. End point reaction: In this type the enzyme reacts with the substrate to form enzyme substrate complex, which in turn gives the product and the enzyme.

$$E + S \longrightarrow ES \longrightarrow P \text{ (Product)} + E \text{ (Enzymes)}$$

2. Reversible reaction: In this case, the enzyme reacts with the substrate to form enzyme substrate complex, which dissociate to form the enzyme and substrate and in some cases the product also formed.

$$E + S \rightleftharpoons ES \longrightarrow P \text{ (Product)} + E \text{ (Enzymes)}$$

3. Temperature dependent reaction: The enzyme activity is very much dependent on the temperature and has a direct effect in which if the temperature is increased the enzyme activity also increased.
4. Time dependent reaction: The intensity of the colour produced after the enzymatic reaction persists for a short time, after which the colour disappears and hence it is important and the optical density is taken as soon as the colour develops (note the time given in the procedure). If time is too much it will lead to erroneous results.

4.1 Estimation of Blood Glucose

Aim: To estimate the amount of glucose present in the given blood sample.

Method: Glucose-Oxidase and Peroxidase (GOD-POD) method.

Principle: Glucose oxidase (GOD) and peroxidase (POD) are used along with chromogen 4-aminoantipyridine and phenol glucose is oxidized by GOD to give D-gluconic acid and hydrogen peroxide. Hydrogen peroxidase in the presence of the enzyme POD oxidizes phenol which combines with 4-aminoantipyridine to give a pink coloured dye and the intensity of the colour developed is directly proportional to the concentration of the substance. The aldehyde group of glucose oxidase gives rise to gluconic acid and hydrogen peroxide. The overall reaction is

$$\text{Glucose} + H_2O + O_2 \longrightarrow \text{Gluconic acid} + H_2O_2$$

The hydrogen peroxide is broken down to water and oxygen by peroxidase.

$$H_2O_2 \xrightarrow{\text{Peroxidase}} H_2O + O_2$$

The oxygen reacts with 4-aminophenazone in the presence of phenol pink-coloured compound and intensity of which can be determined at 540 nm [green filter].

$$O_2 + \text{4-aminophenazone} \longrightarrow \text{Pink-coloured compound}$$

Sample: Fluoride plasma or serum collected within 30 minutes of blood collection.

Reagents

1. Buffer-enzymes: This reagent is prepared by mixing following constituents in 100 ml of phosphate buffer, [M/10.PH 7.0]

A. Glucose oxidase [Sigma]	:	650 units
B. Peroxidase [Sigma]	:	500 units
C. 4-aminophenazone	:	20 mg
D. Sodium azide	:	30 mg

2. Phenol reagent	:	100 mg/dl
3. Glucose standard	:	100 mg/dl

Procedure: Three test tubes are taken and labelled as Blank, Standard and Test. One ml of glucose reagent is added to all the 3 tubes. Then 20 µl of plasma/serum to the 'test' tube is added. 20 µl of glucose standard is added to the standard tube. Finally one ml of distilled water is added to all the 3 tubes. All the tubes are then incubated at room temperature for 15 minutes and read at the optical density at 540 nm.

Normal value

Fasting level	: 80–120 mg/dl
Post prandial	: 120–160 mg/dl

Clinical significance: Increased glucose levels may be found in different conditions such as Diabetes Mellitus, Hyperthyroidism, Hyperpituitarism, Adrenocortical hyper-activity, occasionally in certain hepatic disorders, Pregnancy and Acromegaly, Low glucose levels may be found in different conditions such as tight control of diabetes, overdose of insulin, Hypothyroidism, Hypopituitarism, Hypoadrenalism, Starvation, some drugs e.g. Salicylates and Anti-tuberculosis agents.

4.2 Estimation of Serum Creatinine

Aim: To estimate the amount of creatinine present in the given sample.

Method: Alkaline-picrate method

Name of the reaction: Jaffer's reaction.

Principle: Creatinine in the blood is determined by the reaction with picric acid in an alkaline medium to form a orange coloured tautomers of creatinine picrate. Each volume of centrifuged blood standard creatinine solution of a blank is treated with picric acid and NaOH. The intensity of orange colour is read at 520 nm. From the OD values, concentration of creatinine for 100 ml is calculated.

Sample: Serum.

Reagents

1. Picric acid reagent: 0.91 gm/dl [0.04 M].
2. 10 g/dl, Sodium hydroxide.
3. Working creatinine standards, 1 mg/dl, 5 mg/dl and 10 mg/dl.

The standards are prepared in 0.01 N Hydrochloric acid by using stock creatinine standard 100 mg/dl. Preparation of alkaline picrate reagent: It is prepared fresh by mixing four parts of reagent 1 and one part of reagent 2. This working reagent is stable for one day.

Procedure: Three test tubes are taken and labeled as Blank, Standard and Test. 0.5 ml of reagent 1 is added to all the 3 tubes. 0.2 ml of reagent 2 is added to all the 3 tubes. 0.2 ml of distilled water is added to the 'blank' tube. 0.2 ml of working creatinine standard is added to the 'standard' tube. 0.2 ml of serum is added to the 'test' tube. One ml of distilled water is added to all the 3 test tubes. All the tubes are kept at room temperature for 15 minutes and read at the optical density of 540 nm.

Normal value

Serum creatinine : 0.8–1.4 mg/dl.

Urine creatinine : 1–2 gm in 24 hours Urine specimen.

Clinical significance: Serum creatinine is increased in renal failure. Increased serum creatinine above 1.4 mg/dl is virtually diagnostic of renal failure. Elevated values are also observed in certain other conditions like congestive heart failure, shock and mechanical obstruction of the urinary tract. Serum creatinine levels are unaffected by protein catabolism and external factors. Creatinine clearance is a good measure of the glomerular filtration rate [GFR]. The amount of filtrate made in the kidney depends on the amount of blood present to be filtered and on the ability of the glomeruli to act as a filter. The amount of blood present for filtration is decreased in renal artery arterosclerosis, dehydration and shock. The ability of the glomeruli to act as a filter is decreased by diseases such as glomerulo nephritis, acute tubular necrosis and most other primary renal diseases. Significant bilateral obstruction to ureteric orifice decreases the outflow affecting the GFR. When one of the kidneys is diseased, the opposite kidney if normal has the ability to compensate by increasing its GFR. Therefore, in unilateral kidney disease or postnephrotomy status, a decrease in creatinine clearance is not expected as long as other kidney is normal. Calculation of GFR is done by Cockcroft-Gault formula:

$$\text{Creatinine clearance (ml / mt)} = \frac{(140 - \text{age}) \times \text{lean body weight (Kg)}}{\text{Plasma creatinine (mg/dl)} \times 72}$$

The second method to calculate creatinine clearance is the formula = U × V/P

where, U is number of milligrams/deciliter of creatinine extracted in urine for 24 hours.

V - Volume of urine in milliliter/minute

P - Serum creatinine in milligrams/deciliter.

Normal value

1. Observed value is 78–85 ml/L
2. Corrected value: Multiply the observed value by 1.84 to get the value.

Clinical significance: Increased levels are seen in exercise and pregnancy. Decreased levels are seen in impaired kidney function, acute tubular necrosis, congestive heart failure, shock, dehydration, and cirrhosis with asicitic fluid.

4.3 Estimation of Blood Urea

Aim: To estimate the amount of urea present in unknown blood sample.

Method: Diacetyl monoxime method (DAM).

Principle: Urea reacts with diacetyl-monoxime in hot acetic medium and in the presence of thiosemicarbazide and ferric ions form a pink coloured compound, which can be measured on a green filter.

Reagents

1. **Reagent 1:** [DMR]: It contains 0.2 gm/dl, diacetyl-monoxime in distilled water.
2. **Reagent 2:** [TSC]: It contains 40 mg/dl, thiosemicarbozide in distilled water.
3. **Reagent 3:** [ACID]: It contains 60 ml of concentrated sulphuric acid, 10 ml of orthophosphoric and 10 ml of

1 gm/dl ferric chloride in 1 litre of the reagent prepared in distilled water.

4. **Urea nitrogen standard:** 20 mg/dl: It contains 42.8 mg of urea in 100 ml of saturated benzoic acid.

Preparation of working reagent: It is prepared fresh by mixing one part of reagent 1. One part of reagent 2 and two part of reagent 3. This reagent should be prepared fresh for each batch of the determination.

Precaution: Reagent 3 should be added using Pasteur pipette and it should not be pipetted by mouth since it is highly corrosive.

Procedure: Three test tubes are taken and labeled as Blank, Standard and Test. 0.5 ml of solution I is added to all the 3 tubes. Then 20 µl of plasma/serum to the 'test' tube is added. 20 µl of urea nitrogen standard is added to the standard tube. Two ml of distilled water is added to all the 3 tubes. Finally reagent II is added to all 3 test tubes. All the tubes are kept in a boiling water bath for 10 minutes and read at the optical density [OD] at 540 nm [green filter].

Normal value: Serum urea: 20–40 mg/dl.

Clinical significance: Elevated levels of urea are observed in pre-renal, renal and post-renal uremic conditions. Pre-renal conditions include Diabetic ketoacidosis, dehydration, shock, cardiac failure, haematemesis, severe burns, high fever, reduced blood flow in kidneys, and increased protein catabolism. Renal conditions include diseases of kidneys such as Glomerulonephritis and Tubular Necrosis. Whereas post-renal conditions are enlargement of prostate, stone in the urinary tract and tumor of the bladder. Decreased values are seen in severe liver disease, protein malnutrition, pregnancy (third trimester) and overhydration.

4.4 Estimation of Triglycerides

Aim: To estimate the amount of triglycerides present in the given unknown sample.

Method: Enzymatic method.

Principle: Early clinical method for determining triglycerides involves chemical hydrolysis of a solvent extract of the serum lipids. These methods required preliminary removal of interfering substances like phospholipids. The methods were difficult, slow, provided numerous opportunities for error. They were not readily automotated. The new enzymatic determinations have the following advantages:

1. Mono step methods.
2. Complex reaction within 10-15 minutes.
3. Good reproducibility.
4. Application to automated analyses.
5. Linearity up to 6000 mg/dl, triglycerides concentration.

Chemical principle of test

$$\text{Triglyceride} + H_2O \xrightarrow[\text{Lipoprotein}]{\text{Lipase}} \text{Glycerol} + \text{Fatty acids}$$

$$\text{Glycerol} + \text{ATP} \xrightarrow[\text{Magnesium}]{\text{Glycerol Kinase}} \text{Glycerol-3-phosphate} + \text{ATP}$$

$$\text{Glycerol-3-phosphate} + O_2 \longrightarrow \text{Dihydroxy acetone phosphate} + H_2O_2$$

H_2O_2+ 4 Aminoantipyrine + ADPS (N-ethyl N sulphopropyl-n-methoxyaniline) $\longrightarrow$ Peroxidase red quinone + $4H_2O$, which is proportional to the triglycerides concentration.

Sample: Serum or plasma.

Reagents

1. **Buffer/Enzymes/Chromogen:** It contains (a) Lipoprotein: 30 units, (b) Glycerol Kinase: 10 units, (c) glycerol phosphate oxidase: 5 units, (d) Peroxidase: 5 units, (e) Glycerol phosphate: 100 ml of phosphate buffer, pH: 7.2 (50 M MOL/L).
2. **P-Chlorophenol reagent:** 30 mg/dl.

Preparation of working reagent: It is prepared fresh by mixing two parts of reagent 1 and one part of reagent 2.

Procedure: Three test tubes are taken and labeled as Blank, Standard and Test. One ml of working reagent is added to all the 3 tubes. One ml of distilled water is added to all the 3 tubes. 20 µl of standard reagent is added to the 'standard' tube. 20 µl of serum/plasma is added to the 'test' tube. All the tubes are kept at room temperature for 15 minutes and read at the optical density of 540 nm [green filter].

Normal value: 60–160 mg/dl.

Clinical significance: Elevated levels of triglycerides in plasma has been considered as a risk factor related to Atherosclerotic diseases. The hyperlipidemias can be due to inherited trait or they can be secondary to a variety of disorders or diseases including diabetes mellitus, Biliary obstruction, hypothyroidism, Nephrotic syndrome, Excessive alcohol intake and Familial hypertriglyceridemia and pregnancy. Decreased values are seen in malnutrition, congenital abeta lipoproteinemia.

Additional information: Triglycerides are stored in the adipose tissue by the action of lipoprotein lipase breaking down chylomicrons in the tissue under the influence of insulin. Small amount may be used for energy in the muscle free fatty acids through the blood to the liver. This so-called free fatty acids either enter general carbohydrate metabolism or resynthesized to triglycerides and exported from the liver as VLDL. Estimation should be carried out on the fasting sample. As this will not contain chylomicrons and only a small amount of VLDL is significant for the type of disease that has been classified by Frederickson into five different types. Hyperlipoproteinemia according to Frederickson's classification:

Type I - Very rare ↑ + GL ↑ Chylomicrons

Type II - Common ↑ Total Cholesterol ↑ LDL Cholesterol

Type III - Uncommon ↑ LDL ↑ VLDL ↑ IDL

Type IV - Common ↑ TGL ↑ VLDL

Type V - Uncommon ↑ Chylomicrons ↑ VLDL ↑ TGL

4.5 Estimation of Cholesterol

Aim: To estimate the amount of cholesterol present in the given samples.

Method: Enzymatic method.

Principle: The cholesterol ester hydrolase ester cholester, free cholester is oxidized by the cholestrol oxidase to cholest-4-en-3 one and hydrogen peroxide. Hydrogen peroxide formed reacts with 4-aminoantipyrine and phenol in the presence of peroxidase to produce a pink coloured quinoneimine dye. The intensity of the colour produced is proportion to the amount of cholesterol present in the sample.

$$\text{Cholesterol ester} + H_2O \xrightarrow{\text{Cholesterol esterase}} \text{Cholesterol} + \text{Fattyacids}$$

$$\text{Cholesetrol} + O_2 \longrightarrow \text{Cholest-4-en-3 one} + H_2O$$

$$H_2O\text{+4-Aminoantipyrine} + \text{Phenol} \longrightarrow \text{Quinoneimine red dye} + H_2O$$

Sample: Serum or heparinised plasma.

Reagents

1. Buffer/Enzyme/Chromogen: It contain cholesterol hydrogen: 10 units, cholesterol: 15 units and peroxidase: 3500 units, dissolved in 100 ml of phosphate buffer (M/L, Ph 7.0) containing 50 mg of 4-aminophenozone and 30 mg sodium azide.
2. Phenol: 30 mg/dl in distilled water.
3. Cholesterol standard: 200 mg/dl.

Preparation of working reagent: It is prepared fresh by mixing two parts of reagent 1 and one part of reagent 2.

Procedure: Three test tubes are taken and labeled as Blank, Standard and Test. One ml of working reagent is added to all the 3 tubes. One ml of distilled water is added to all the 3 tubes. 20 μl of standard reagent is added to the 'standard' tube. 20 μl of serum/plasma is added to the 'test' tube. All the tubes are kept at room temperature for 15 minutes and read at the optical density of 540 nm [green filter].

Normal value: Serum cholesterol: 130–250 mg/dl.

Clinical significance: Elevated or increased levels are seen in Idiopathic hypercholesterimia, Obstructive jaundice, Hypothyroidism, Atherosclerosis, obesity, Xanthomatous disorder, Familial hyperlipoproteinemias, Hyperlipedemia, Nephrotic syndrome and Cirrhosis, Coronary artery disease, and pregnancy. Decreased levels are seen in severe liver disease, Hyperthyroidism, Chronic anaemia, Tangier's disease, Malabsorption, Malnutrition, A-beta lipoproteinemia, some drugs e.g. Nicotinic acid and Statin's reduce serum cholesterol levels. Very high level of cholesterol is associated with increased risk of Coronary artery disease.

4.6 Estimation of HDL Cholesterol

Aim: To estimate the amount of HDL cholesterol present in the given samples.

Method: Polyethylene glycol 6000.

Principle: Low density lipoprotein (LDL) very low density lipoprotein (VLDL) are precipitated by a solution polyethylene glycol 6000 leaving behind the high density lipoprotein (HDL).

Sample: Serum.

Reagents: Cholesterol reagent 1, Cholesterol reagent 2.

These two reagents are the same as used in the determination of total cholesterol.

Additional reagents:

1. Phosphotungstic acid reagent (PTA).
2. Magnesium chloride reagent.
3. Cholesterol reagent.

Precaution: Do not use lipaemic specimen (cloudy or milky) which will give rise to false elevated values.

Procedure: Take equal amount of sample and polyethylene glycol, shake well and keep it at room temperature for 10 minutes. Then centrifuge at 3000 rpm for 15 minutes to obtain a clear supernatant. Three test tubes are taken and labeled as Blank, Standard and Test. One ml of cholesterol reagent is added to all the 3 tubes. One ml of distilled water is added to all the 3 tubes. 100 µl of supernatant from the sample is added to the 'test' tube, 100 µl cholesterol standard reagent is added to the 'standard' tube. All the tubes are kept at room temperature for few minutes and read at the optical density of 540 nm [green filter].

Normal value

Less than 19 years—Female	:	30–70 mg/dl.
Male	:	30–65 mg/dl.
40 years and above—Female	:	30–85 mg/dl.
Male	:	30–70 mg/dl.

Clinical significance: The increase in total cholesterol is generally associated with ischaemic heart disease. HDL Cholesterol concentration, however negatively correlates well with the risk of IHD (Ischaemic heart disease), and is widely accepted as the best single protector of heart. HDL concentration below 45 mg/dl in female and 35 mg/dl in male is considered as increased risk of IHD.

4.7 Estimation of Acid Phosphatase

Aim: To estimate the amount of acid phosphatase present in the given samples.

Method: King and Armstrong method.

Principle: Acid phosphatase from serum converts phenyl phosphate to inorganic phosphate and phenol at pH 4.9. The phenol so formed reacts in the alkaline medium with 4-amino antipyrine in the presence of oxidizing agent (4-potassium ferricyanide) and forms a orange-red coloured complex which can be read calorimetrically. Since tartarate inhibits the prostatic fraction of the enzyme the difference in acid phosphatase activity with and without tartarate represents the activity of the prostatic fraction.

Nitrophenol phosphate + H_2O $\xrightarrow{\text{Acid phosphatase}}$ Phenol + disodium hydrogen PO_4

Phenol + 4-aminoantipyrine potassium ferricyanide $\longrightarrow$ red coloured complex

Sample: Fresh serum specimen must be free from haemolysis. The enzyme is unstable at room temperature.

Two-three drops of 6 M acetic acid per 5 ml of serum can stabilize the enzyme. Under such conditions the enzyme may remain stable.

Reagents

1. Solution 1 (Buffered substrate)
2. Working standard
3. Tartarate stable
4. Sodium hydroxide
5. Sodium bicarbonate
6. Solution 2 (4-amino-antipyrine)
7. Solution 3 (potassium ferricyanide)

Procedure: Five test tubes are taken and labeled as Blank, Standard, Test, control and tartarate stable standard. 0.5 ml of Solution 1 (Buffered substrate) is added in 'control', 'test' 'Tartarate stable' test tubes. 1.1 ml of distilled water to the 'Blank', 0.6 ml to the 'standard' and 0.5 ml to the 'control', 'test' and 'tartarate stable', mixed well and incubated at 37°C for 3 minutes. One ml of working reagent is added to all the 3 tubes. One ml of distilled water is added to all the 3 tubes. 0.5 ml of working standard reagent is added to the 'standard' tube. One drop tartarate tartrate stable reagent is added to the tartarate stable. It was left for 60 minutes at room temperature. 0.5 ml of sodium hydroxide is added to all the 5 tubes. 0.5 ml sodium bicarbonate is added to all the 5 tubes. 0.5 ml of sodium 2 (potassium ferricyanide) is added to all the 5 tubes. After 10 minutes the optical density was recorded at 540 nm.

Normal value

Serum total acid phosphatase : 1.0–4.0 KA units.

Prostatic fraction : 0–0.8 KA units.

Clinical significance: Elevations of the acid phosphatase are found in the sera of the males with prostatic cancer with metastases. Increased values are seen in Prostatic carcinoma, Pagets disease, Hyperparathyroidism, Metastasis of the bone, Chronic renal failure, Multiple myeloma, Sickle cell crisis,

Renal impairment, Cirrhosis, Haemolytic anemia Gaucher's disease. Decreased values are seen in overhydration.

REFERENCES

Gerhard Meisenberg, William H. Simmons, 2006. *Principles of Medical Biochemistry*, Elsevier Science Health Science Division.

Kent E. Vrana, 1999. *Biochemistry*, Lippincott Williams and Wilkins.

Luxton, R., C.J. Pallister, 1999. *Clinical Biochemistry*, Cold Spring Harber Laboratory Pr.

Michael A. Lieberman, Dawn B. Marks, Allan D. Marks, Colleen Smith, Marks, 2006. *Essential Medical Biochemistry*, Lippincott Williams and Wilkins.

Pamela C. Champe, Richard A. Harvey, Denis R. Ferrier, 2007. *Biochemistry*, Lippincott Williams and Wilkins.

Simon W. Walker, Poter Ashhy, Peter Rae, 2005. *Clinical Biochemistry*, Blackwell Publications.

Spiegel, H., 1984. *Clinical Biochemistry, Contemporary Theories and Techniques*, Academic Press.

Thomas M. Devlin, 2005. *Textbook of Biochemistry—with clinical correlation*, John Wiley and Sons Inc.

Varley, H., 1988. *Practical Clinical Biochemistry*, CBS, New Delhi.

Vikas Bhushan, Tao Le, Vishal Pall, 2005. *Biochemistry*, Lippincott Williams.

5

Histopathological Techniques

5.1 Histology

Histology is the microscopic study of normal tissues; and histopathology is the study of abnormal or diseased tissues. This division of medical laboratory science is once referred to as morbid anatomy. At present, many workers prefer to call it cellular pathology, cytology. The study of cells is an integral part of histopathology and in most histological preparations, the components of individual cells are studied. Most of histopathological techniques are applied to killed tissues which have been fixed in such a way that they retain their structures and components as closely as possible to those of living tissues.

There are various techniques and methods designed and employed in histopathological investigations as it is impossible to study all normal and abnormal tissue components in a single preparation of thin sections enables separate sections to be studied and stained in a variety of ways. However, a good knowledge of the structures of cells, organs and tissues is essential for the study to be worthwhile.

- Histology is the microscopic study of the normal tissue of the body.
- Pathology is the study of structural and functional changes in the tissues and organs of the body which are caused by the disease.
- Histopathology is the microscopic study of the tissue affected by the disease.
- Histopathological technique: The procedures adopted for preparation of materials for such

(histopathological) studies are known as histological or histopathological technique.

- Tissue is made up of collections of normal cells.
- Biopsy is a piece of tissue removed from the living organism. For example skin biopsy, lymph node biopsy, it is usually done in operation theatres (OT) and specimen must be immediately put in fixative.

Types of Biopsy

1. Aspiration or fine needle aspiration biopsy
2. Cone biopsy
3. Core needle biopsy
4. Vacuum assisted core biopsy
5. Endoscopic biopsy
6. Punch biopsy
7. Surface biopsy
8. Surgical biopsy or excisional biopsy.

Autopsy (Necropsy): It is the examination of the body after its death. It is done in the post-mortem room to find out the cause for the death.

The functions of pathology technician are:

1. To prepare tissue section from biopsy or autopsy to slide, which is examined by pathologist.
2. Responsible to the patient (maintaining the proper number, labeling and register).
3. To serve the patients.

Handling and Reception of Specimen

1. After biopsy is taken from the body, it should be handled carefully to prevent crush injury to the tissue. Unnecessary use of forceps to hold the tissue has to be avoided.
2. It is then placed immediately into the fixatives. A wide mouthed bottle is chosen to removed the specimen easily in the laboratory.

3. The volume of fixatives should be at least 15-20 times higher than the volume of the tissue.
4. The bottle should be labeled (not in washable ink) with name and hospital number of the patient, date of biopsy and nature of the specimen.
5. The bottle is then closed with a well fitted cap to ensure that no fixative leaks out.
6. In case the specimen has to be sent to a distant laboratory the bottle cap is further reinforced with adhesive plaster and the bottle has to be packed well in a cardboard box and mailed to the laboratory along with the request form giving clinical details of the patient.

On Reception of the Specimen

1. The name and hospital number of the patient. Date of biopsy and the nature of specimen as mentioned on the bottle have to be matched with the details given in the accompanying form.
2. Ensure that the specimen is intact in the bottle and has not been lost in transit to the laboratory.
3. Ensure that there is sufficient fixative in the bottle and that it has not leaked out. If it has leaked out then pour sufficient fixative in the bottle and allow further fixation of the tissue.
4. Make an entry of the relevant details in the lab register and assign a biopsy number to the specimen.
5. A gross description of specimen including its size, shape and other special characters is to be noted either immediately or after completing fixation of the specimen.
6. Larger specimens are usually cut into smaller pieces to enable proper penetration of the fixative and for the good fixation of the tissue.
7. After careful examination and description of the tissue, the representative pieces from fixed tissue are taken and send it for processing.

8. Samples of the information that may be entered in the register are as given below:
   - Serial number
   - Biopsy number
   - Date of receipt of specimen
   - IP number and name
   - Age
   - Sex
   - Ward specimen
   - Fixative gross
   - Date of description
   - Microscopic description
   - Diagnosis of specimen
   - Date of reporting
   - Date of discarding.

There are different methods of preparing tissue for microscopic examination like teased preparation, squash preparation smears, impression smears, frozen section, etc.

The best and the most effective means of studying normal and diseased tissue of the body microscopically is by the examination of thin sections (one cell thick) of fixed tissue appropriately stained to distinguish different cells and pattern. Making thin slices of fixed tissue usually produces these sections. Fixation is necessary to prevent post-mortem changes, which occur shortly after death or on removal of specimen from the body.

Prior to sectioning the fixed tissue is usually embedded in a solid medium, which facilitates easy cutting of the section. Paraffin wax is the most widely used embedding medium for preparing histological slides. Paraffin wax embedding permits thin individual and serial sections to be cut with easily from a majority of tissues. It also allows a multitude of staining techniques to be employed and it facilitates the storage of blocks and unstained sections.

The various steps involved in the preparation of tissue for histological examination are:

1. Fixation
2. Processing and embedding
3. Sections cutting and
4. Staining

5.2 Fixation

Fixation is the preservation after death of the shape, structure and chemical constituents of tissues and cells. Soon after death, tissues and cells begin to undergo changes leading to their break down and ultimate destruction. Such changes may be due to the action of enzymes normally present in the tissues themselves and so the changes are termed autolytic action.

Autolysis is a self-destructive process due to the release of autolytic enzymes from the dead cell.

Purification: It is a decomposition and death of tissue due to the action of bacteria that invades the tissue (foul smelling and gas production).

In order to make a proper histological study of the tissue post-mortem changes should be arrested and the tissue has to be preserved as close as possible to the living state. This is made possible by the use of fixatives.

Fixation is defined as substance, which prevents post-mortem changes and preserves the morphological and chemical characteristics of cells and tissue.

Action of fixative: Fixative acts by coagulating protein in the tissue, through the formation of cross-links between protein molecules thereby keeping their relation to each other. (This is very much like the coagulation of albumin in the white of an egg.) When heated it destroys the enzymes and bacteria thereby prevents autolysis and putrefaction.

Preservation: To keep the tissue in its original structure as it is in the living body.

Hardening: It helps the process of cutting. It is easier to make thin section if the tissue is hard.

Objectives of Fixation

- To prevent autolysis
- To prevent putrefaction
- To preserve and harden the tissue
- To improve the staining
- To help permeation of staining into the tissue.

Procedure for Fixation

1. The amount of fixative must be 15-20 or 10-15 times larger than the volume of the tissue.
2. The tissue should be smaller piece. Fluid used in the processing penetrates the tissue well if it is thin and small.
3. The duration of fixation is 6-48 hours but generally with average tissues, the fixation is completed within 24 hours.

The factors deciding the duration:

Fixation depends upon:

(a) Size of tissue—big—longer duration.

(b) Density of tissue—e.g. loose tissue, fat—less time, hard tissue—more time.

(c) Penetration of fixatives used.

(d) Temperature of fixatives, more the temperature, faster the fixation. (Minimum 6 hours may be used by agitating the tissue by keeping in rotator fitted with motor.)

Types of Fixatives

A. Simple fixatives

(i) Formaldehyde, Mercuric chloride, Picric acid, Osmium tetroxide, Acetic acid, Ethyl alcohol, Potassium dichromate, Chromic acid.

B. Microanatomical fixative

1. Formalin fixative:
   - (a) 10% formalin
   - (b) 10% formal saline
   - (c) 10% neutral formalin
   - (d) Calcium acetate formalin (Lillie's fixative)
2. Zenker's fixative (Mercuric chloride fixative)
3. Halley's fixative (Zenker's formal)
4. FMA fixative (after Lowy)
5. Bouin's fixative
   - (i) Nuclear fixative—Carnoy's fixative
   - (ii) Cytoplasmic fixatives—Flemming's fluid.

C. Fixation of smears

1. Alcohol-ether
2. Schaudinn's fluid
3. Aerosol spray fixatives
4. 95% ethyl or methyl alcohol.

Formalin fixative

Formalin is a 40% formaldehyde gas dissolved in water. Formaldehyde gas dissolves in water only up to a maximum of 40% by weight. So for all practical purposes the 40% solution is considered as concentrated formalin.

Formaldehyde is in polymerized form in formalin and it is not suitable for fixation. It is diluted to 10% formalin when depolymerization occurs and it becomes suitable for fixation. Formalin fixatives are the most commonly used fixatives in histopathology either alone or in combination with other fixatives.

General advantages of formalin fixatives:

- It is cheap.
- It is relatively easy to prepare.
- It is quite stable (when buffered).

- It permits many staining procedures.
- It penetrates the tissue rapidly.
- It does not cause excessive hardening of the tissue.
- Frozen section can be made with formalin fixed tissue.
- Tissue can be kept in formalin for longer period without being hardened. (E.g. Museum specimen)
- It preserves loose tissue well. (E.g. Fatty tissue).
- It allows the study of some tissue enzymes.
- It is ideal for mailing the specimen after adequate fixation (for transport no need to maintain 10 times of the volume of tissue).
- It is the best fixative for nervous system.

Disadvantages of formalin:

- Formalin is unpleasant.
- Direct contact of formalin with skin produces allergy and dermatitis of hands for some people. Wearing gloves while handling the formalin prevents it.
- It fumes irritate eyes and nose.
- It forms pigment called formalin pigment (formic acid, dark brown artifact pigment) especially with unbuffered formalin and if the tissue contains blood, buffered formalin can be used to prevent formalin pigment.
- It causes shrinkage of collagen (so not suitable for skin biopsies).
- It forms white precipitate of para formaldehyde, which is prevented by adding methanol.

a. 10% formalin:

Composition: Full strength formalin

(40% formaldehyde) – 10 ml

Distilled water – 90 ml

b. 10% formal saline:

Composition: Full strength formalin – 100 ml

NaCl	–	9 ml
Distilled water	–	900 ml

It is used for fixation of general surgical specimen biopsies and tissues from CNS.

c. **Neutral Formalin:**

It is prepared by adding calcium carbonates (marbles) to 100 ml of formalin.

d. 10% neutral buffered formalin:

Full strength formalin	–	100 ml
Sodium dihydrogen phosphate (anhydrous)	–	4 gm
Disodium hydrogen phosphate (anhydrous)	–	6.5 gm
Distilled water	–	900 ml
It contains both acid and alkali (buffer) pH	–	7.2

Advantages

1. It prevents the formation of formalin pigments.
2. It maintains pH during processing and staining.

Uses

- Formalin is used for research, surgical and postmortem specimens.
- It is prepared and stored in large bottles of which the bottom is a one inch layer of marble chips (calcium carbonate).

Zenker's Fluid:

Compound fixative, mercuric chloride fixative.

Formula

Potassium dichromate	-	2.5 gm
Mercuric chloride	-	6.0 gm
Distilled water	-	10 ml

Working solution: To add 5 ml of glacial acetic acid to 100 ml of Zenker's fluid just before use.

Advantages

1. Zenker's fluid rapidly penetrates the tissue and permits excellent staining of nuclei and connective tissue.
2. It produces less shrinkage.

Disadvantages

1. It has the disadvantage of hardening of the tissues and leaving behind mercuric precipitates in the tissues, which require prolonged washing to remove.
2. Iodine is added during staining to remove mercuric chloride.

Helly's fluid (Zenker Formal)

By adding the formalin to Zenker's fluid the beneficial effects of both fixative are combined, minimizing their disadvantages.

Formula

Zenker's fluid + 5 cc full strength formalin = Helley's fluid

K Dichromate	- 2.5 gm
Mercuric chloride	- 6.0 gm
Distilled water	- 100 ml
Formalin full strength	- 5.0 ml

It stains nucleus, cytoplasm and connective tissue well.

It is recommended for bone marrow and blood containing tissue.

FMA Fixative

Formula

Full strength formalin	- 100 ml
Mercuric chloride	- 20 gm
Acetic acid glacial	- 50 ml
D.H_2O	- 100 ml
Duration of Fixation	- 2-3 hours

Carnoy's Fixative

Formula

Absolute ethanol	- 600 ml
Chloroform	- 300 ml
Glacial acetic acid	- 100 ml

Uses: It is used to demonstrate chromosomes, glycogen in tissues and urgent biopsies.

Duration of fixation: one hour.

Leaving the alcohol fixative for a long time leads to excessive hardening and shrinkage of tissue.

Bouin's Fluid

Formula

Saturated picric acid	- 75 ml
Full strength formalin	- 25 ml
Glacial acetic acid	- 5.0 ml

- Bouin's fluid contains picric acid, a dye and stains the tissue yellow.
- It is recommended for testicular biopsies and fixation of embryo.

Compound fixative: 10% buffered formalin, Zenker's fluid, Zenker formal, Bouin's fluid.

Decalcification: The deposition of calcium salts (calcium phosphate, calcium carbonate and calcium fluorite), usually makes the cutting of fine sections by the usual methods, very difficult. The removal of these calcium salts is known as decalcification. The most suitable method of decalcification depends on the strength, temperature and volume of the decalcifying solution as well as on the size, consistency of the tissue and type of investigation to be carried out. Calcium salts occur normally in bones and teeth or in some pathological condition.

Decalcifying Solutions and Agents

1. Aqueous formic acid
2. Aqueous nitric acid
3. Perenyi's fluid
4. Ebner's fluid
5. Ion exchange resins
6. Electrolytic decalcification
7. Ultrasonic decalcification

5.3 Tissue Processing and Embedding

The stepwise treatment of tissue that ultimately results in impregnation of tissue with solid medium like paraffin wax is called tissue processing. Most of fixatives used routinely are aqueous fixatives. Paraffin wax cannot directly impregnate the tissues fixed in these aqueous fixatives because they are not miscible.

Types of Embedding

1. Paraffin wax
2. Celloidin or low viscosity nitrocellulose
3. Gelatin embedding
4. Plastic embedding
5. Various types of resins; or by freezing.

After fixation the sequence of events in tissue processing are:

1. Dehydration
2. Clearing
3. Wax impregnation.

5.4 Dehydration

The process of removal of water from the tissue is called dehydration. Complete removal of water from the tissue is necessary for processing because it does not mix with paraffin. Two solutions commonly used in dehydration are:

1. Alcohol
2. Acetone.

Alcohol: It is commonly used:

(a) Ethyl alcohol—expensive.

(b) Isopropyl alcohol—less expensive and commonly used.

Gradual dehydration is necessary, directly putting the tissue into absolute alcohol produces rapid dehydration but results in hardening and distortion of the tissue.

For example: 70%, 80%, 95%, 100% alcohol.

Clearing (De-alcoholization)

Clearing agents are the one which allows mixing with paraffin. Dehydrating agents such as alcohol and acetone do not mix with paraffin. So, clearing agent is used. During clearing, alcohol in the tissue is replaced by a fluid that will dissolve the wax into which the tissue is to be impregnated.

Action

1. De-alcoholization (removal of alcohol)
2. Mixing with paraffin

   (a) **Xylene:** It is a rapidly clearing agent (15-30 min.) and tissues tend to become hardened and brittle if it is left in xylene for longer periods.

   (b) **Chloroform:** It is less harmful and causes minimal shrinkage or hardening of tissue. It is slower in action and tissue takes 6-24 hours for complete clearing.

   (c) Cedar wood oil—It is rarely used.

5.5 Wax Impregnation or Infiltration

Infiltration is the process of placing the paraffin into the tissues.

*E.g.*1. Paraffin
   2. Celloidin
   3. Carbo wax-water soluble
   4. Beewax.

Paraffin

1. It filtrates the tissues
2. It supports the tissue
3. It encloses the tissue or cell.

Properties of embedding medium

1. It should be liquid at reasonable temperature and becomes solid at room temperature.

2. It should be capable of being converted from liquid to solid form readily and reasonably within room temperature.
3. Beeswax is added to the paraffin to get good section.
4. The melting temperature is 50°C to 60°C called hard paraffin.
5. Two changes of paraffin are used to remove traces of clearing agents. Presence of small amounts of clearing agent makes the block very soft.
6. Paraffin I – 1 to 2 hours.

   Paraffin II – 12 hours (overnight)—to remove traces of clearing agents.
7. Melting temperature should not be above 65°C and accepted temperature during process is 56°C.

The processing can be done either manually or using an automatic tissue-processing machine called Histokinette.

5.6 Hand Processing

1.	95% Alcohol I	08.00 – 09.00 a.m.	1 hr
2.	95% Alcohol II	09.00 – 10 a.m.	1 hr
3.	Acetone I	10.00 – 11 a.m.	1 hr
4.	Acetone II	11.00 – 12 noon	1 hr
5.	Chloroform I	12.00 – 01.00 p.m.	1 hr
6.	Chloroform II	01.00 – 02.00 p.m.	1 hr
7.	Paraffin I	02.00 – 03.00 p.m.	1 hr
8.	Paraffin II	03.00 – 04.00 p.m.	1 hr

Embed at 4 p.m. or the following morning.

5.7 Automatic Processing

1.	70% Alcohol I	04.30	06.30 p.m.	2 hrs
2.	70% Alcohol II	06.30	07.00 p.m.	half an hr
3.	70% Alcohol III	07.00	08.00 p.m.	1 hr
4.	95% Alcohol I	08.00	09.00 p.m.	1 hr
5.	95% Alcohol II	09.00	10.00 p.m.	1 hr
6.	Acetone I	10.00	12.00 mid noon	2 hrs
7.	Acetone II	12.00	01.00 a.m.	1 hr
8.	Acetone III	01.00	02.00 a.m.	1 hr
9.	Chloroform I	02.00	04.00 a.m.	2 hrs
10.	Chloroform II	04.00	05.00 a.m.	1 hr
11.	Paraffin I	05.00	06.00 a.m.	1 hr
12.	Paraffin II	06.00	08.00 a.m.	2 hrs

5.8 Section Cutting

Having fixed, processed and embedded the tissue, the next stage is to cut sections from the block. The machines or instruments used to cut thin sections are called microtomes.

Microtome is an instrument designed for accurate cutting of thin section of tissue.

Types of Microtome

1. Rotary microtome—commonly used
2. Rocking microtome
3. Base sledge microtome
4. Sliding microtome
5. Freezing microtome (for emergency)
6. Cryostat: In this whole microtome with knife is inside the freezer. It is used for emergency and makes the block and slides within 15 minutes. Sections are used

for staining fat and glycogen (these are dissolved during processing).

7. Ultramicrotome.

Rotary microtome: It is an excellent instrument for the production of serial sections.

Major parts of microtome:

- Block holder
- Knife
- Adjustment screws
- Operating handle (fly wheel).

Microtome Knife

Microtome knives are available in various sizes. They are classified based on their blade profiles: (a) Plane wedge, (b) Planoconcave, (c) Wedge-shaped, (d) Biconcave and (e) Tool edge profiles.

Knife is the most important for sectioning and it is important for microtome.

Honing guide: It makes uniform bevel during sharpening. It gives proper angle to edge of knife when it is sharpened by hand.

Types of Microtome Knives

1. **Plane wedge**
    - This is the most commonly used microtome knife, especially in rotary microtome. It is convenient for routine sectioning.
    - It is easy to sharpen.
    - It is recommended for cutting frozen sections, paraffin sections and hard tissues embedded in celloidin.
2. **Plano concave:** One surface of the knife is plane surface and the other is concave. It is used for cutting celloidin embedded tissues.

3. **Biconcave:** This knife is concave on both surfaces. It is used to cut wax embedded tissue and is more often used in the rocking microtome.
4. **Tool edge:** This type of knife is plane on both sides with a steep cutting edge. It is used on robust microtomes for cutting hard tissues such as undecalcified bone.

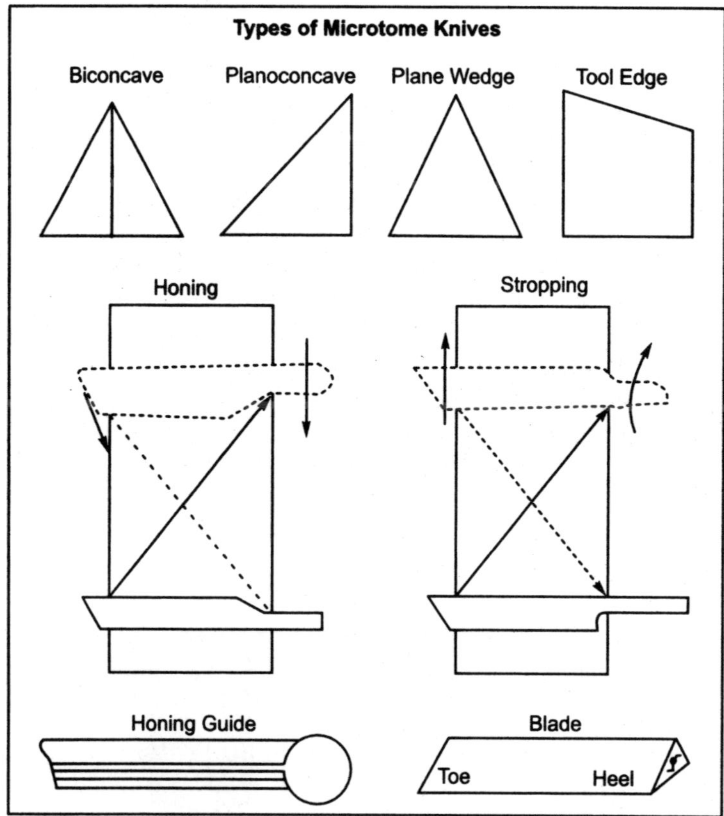

Microtome Knife Angle

The angle formed at the actual cutting edge is called the facet or cutting or 'bevel' angle and the sides of the knife enclosing this angle is called cutting facets or the bevel. This is especially important because during manual sharpening of the knife it is the cutting facets that need to be sharpened and not the rest of the knife surface. The angle between the cutting facet and the block of the tissue is called the clearance angle. A clearance angle of 2-6 is found to be optimum to prevent friction between the block and the knife.

Sharpening microtome knives: The microtome knife should be sharpened whenever the cutting edge becomes blunt or damaged. Sharpening is done by 2 methods.

1. Manually or
2. Automatic knife sharpening machine.

Honing: The hone is then covered with a thin film of lubricant such as soap-water. The actual process of sharpening the knife-edge is referred to as honing.

Stropping: The process of polishing of the knife-edge is called stropping.

Honing is done to remove nicks from the knife. A sharp knife is indispensable and it is most important for entire section cutting process. It is performed manually using a rectangular block of natural or synthetic stone called hone. The hone is graded coarse medium and fine according to the particle size it is made up of and its abrasiveness.

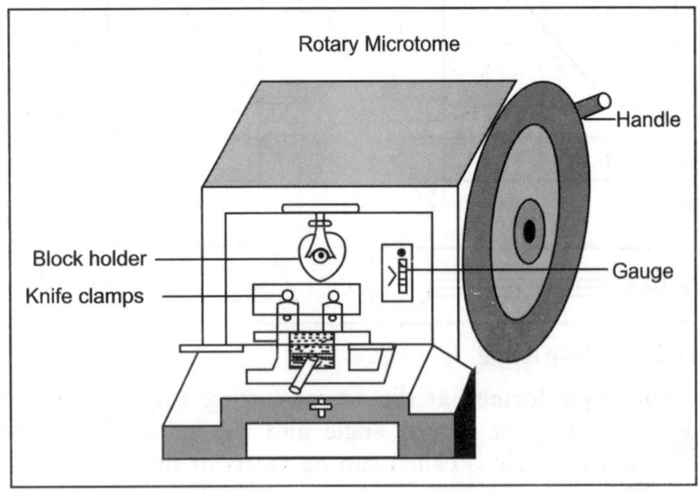

Procedure for Honing (Heel to toe)

1. Clean the knife with xylene and attach the knife handle and honing guide.
2. Clean the surface of hone with xylene to remove the dust from its surface.
3. Lubricate the surface of hone with oil or soap water.
4. Place the knife on the near end of the hone and move forward diagonally with the cutting edge leading.
5. Turn the knife on its back after reading the end of the stone and the knife is drawn diagonally back again with the cutting edge leading.

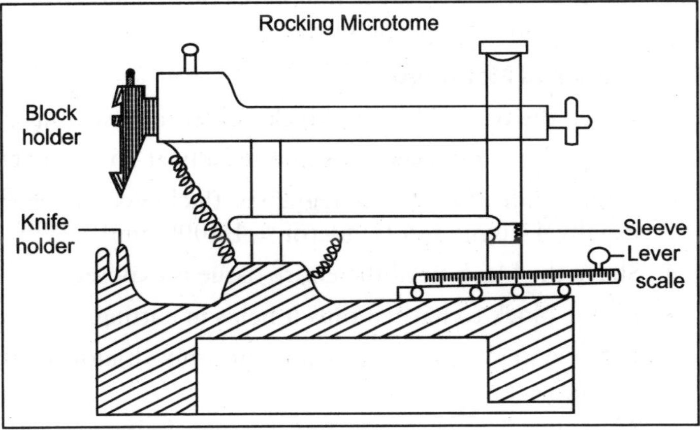

The number of stroke required depends on the bluntness of knife edge. But in general honing is complete when all large nicks are removed and the edge is straight and sharp.

The duration of sharpening = 15-30 min.

Testing of Knife

1. By looking at the knife-edge under the low power of microscope—no nicks should be seen.
2. The sharpened knife has to split the hair.

Stropping

Stropping is the process of polishing and cleaning of knife-edge on softer material like leather strop that is usually obtained from the horse hide. It is performed in a manner similar to that of honing except that the knife is reversed, with the back of knife leading (cutting edge trailing) and the movement being from toe to heel.

Maintenance of Knife

1. Must be kept dry and oily (presence of H_2O leads to rusting).
2. Protect the knife edge at all time by suspending the knife so that the edges do not touch anything.

Section Cutting and Mounting

Trimming: Trim the block to leave minimum paraffin around the tissues. Then attach the block with small wooden or metal block and number the block.

5.9 Cutting and Mounting

- Fasten the tissue block to block holder in microtome.
- Fix the knife in proper position usually at 35-45° angle.
- Adjust indicator which regulates thickness of section usually 4-10 micron (1 micron = 1/1000 mm).
- Shave the block until the entire tissue is exposed.
- Ice the block to harden thus it helps in cutting.
- Revolve the wheel with a even and smooth motion and cut the section.
- Take the section with brush from knife and float it in constant water bath (45 to 50°C) to remove and stretches out wrinkles. (The temperature of water should be maintained at 5-10°C below the melting point of wax in use.)
- Take clean well-washed slide coated with egg albumin.
- Keep the slide in upright position for few seconds to drain water.
- Place the slide on a warming table for few minutes to remove water.

- Transfer the slide to paraffin oven and keep it for 40 min–4 hrs, at 45°C to ensure that the section is fixed to the slide and is dry and ready for staining.

5.10 Haematoxylin and Eosin Staining

Aim: To perform the Haematoxylin and Eosin staining for the given tissue sample.

Principle: Haematoxylin and eosin are the principal stains used for the demonstration of nucleus, and the cytoplasmic inclusion. Alum acts as a mordant and haematoxylin containing alum stains the nucleus light blue which turns red in the presence of acid. The cell differentiation is achieved by treating the tissue with acid solution. Using eosin solution, which imparts pink colour to cytoplasm, performs the counter staining.

Reagent required

1. **Harris's Haematoxylin stain**

   Haematoxylin crystal – 1 gm
   Alcohol 95% – 10 ml
   Ammonium or potassium alum – 20 gm
   Distilled water – 200 ml
   Mercuric oxide – 0.5 gm

2. **Eosin solution**

   Eosin – 1 gm
   Distilled water – 80 ml
   95% alcohol – 320 ml
   Glacial acetic acid – 0.4 ml

3. **Dilute aqueous hydrochloric acid**

   Con. HCl – 2.5 ml
   Distilled water – 500 ml

4. **Dilute ammonia water**

   Strong ammonia – 1.5 ml
   Distilled water – 500 ml

Procedure

- Deparaffinise the section.
- Treat the section with xylene immediately after taking it out from the drying oven.
- Report the xylene treatment with agitation – 1 minute.
- Treat the section to water through down-graded alcohol bath for 30-60 seconds (100%, 90%, 70%).
- Wash it in the running tap water, rinse it in the distilled water, drain well, stain it with Harris's haematoxylin for 5 minutes.
- Wash in the running tap water. Quickly dip the slide in and out of .5 per cent hydrochloride acid.
- Wash briefly in water for 30-60 seconds.
- Dip it several times in the dilute ammonia water, the section will change into blue colour.
- Wash in water.
- Rinse in 95 per cent alcohol.
- Agitate it in eosin staining solution for 1-2 minutes.
- Dehydration, clearing and mounting.

Result

Nucleus – Blue colour

Erythrocytes – Red colour.

Muscle, Cytoplasm, Connective tissue – Shades of pink colour.

5.11 Other Staining Procedures

1. Staining for Amyloid

(Benhold's Congo red stain)

Aim: To perform the amyloidal staining for a given tissue sample.

Principle: Alkali alcoholic solvent or using competitive inhibition by salt solution had the effect of suppressing the electrochemical staining of other tissue components, enhance the hydrogen bondings and so improving selectivity for amyloids.

Reagents

1. Mayers's haematoxylin
   - Haematoxylin – 1 gm
   - Sodium iodide – 0.2 gm
   - Ammonium or Potassium alum – 50 gm
   - Citric acid – 1 gm
   - Distilled water – 100 ml
2. Sodium chloride ethanol solution:
   - 1 gm of sodium chloride in 100 ml of ethanol
3. 1 per cent sodium hydroxide solution.
4. Alkalin alcohol sodium chloride solution:
   - Sodium chloride ethanol solution – 50 ml
   - 1 per cent sodium hydroxide – 0.5 ml
5. Stock congo red solution:
   - Sodium chloride ethanol solution – 300 ml
   - Congo red – 0.5 gm
6. Working congo red solution:
   - Stock congo red solution – 50 ml
   - 1 gm sodium hydroxide – 0.5 ml

Mix well and filter and used within 15 minutes.

Procedure

- Deparaffinise the section.
- Take the section to water.
- Stain with Mayers's haematoxylin for 10 minutes.
- Wash in running warm water for 5-10 minutes.
- Rinse in distilled water.
- Treat with alkaline alcohol sodium chloride solution for 20 minutes.
- Treat with working congo red solution for 15-20 minutes.
- Dehydrate, clear and mount.

Result: Amyloid – Deep pink or red colour
Nuclei – Blue colour.

Periodic acid – Schiff stain

2. Staining for Carbohydrate

Principle: The principle of the reaction is the periodic acid will bring about oxidative cleavage of the carbon to carbon bond in 1, 2 glycols or their amino or alkyl aminoderivative to form dialdehydes. These aldehydes will react with fuchsin sulfurous acid which combine with basic-fuchsin to form a magenta colour compound.

Reagents

1. 1% periodic acid:

Periodic acid	– 1 gm
Distilled water	– 100 ml

2. Schiff's reagent

Warm distilled water	– 1000 ml
Basic-fuchsin	– 5 gm

3. | | |
   |---|---|
   | Concentrated HCl | – 8.35 ml |
   | Distilled water | – 91.65 ml |

4. Light green counter stain:

Light green	– 100 mg
Acetic acid (0.1%)	– 100 ml

Procedure

1. Keep the slides in xylene for 15 minutes.
2. Wash in graded alcohol (absolute, 90%, 80%) each 2 dips.
3. Wash in water.
4. Place in periodic acid for 15 minutes.
5. Wash in water.
6. Place in Schiff's reagent for 15 minutes.
7. Wash in water for 10 minutes.

8. Stain in haematoxylin for 3 minutes.
9. Wash in water.
10. Differentiate in 1% acid alcohol (3 dips).
11. Wash in water.
12. Blueing in light green for a few dips.
13. Wash in water.
14. Dehydrate, clear and mount the slide.

Result: Glycogen, mucin, reticulin, basement membrane, amyloids, and other element may show a positive reaction—Rose to Purple red.

Nuclei – Blue

Fungi – Red

Verhoeff's elastic stain

Principle: Elastic fibers are highly crosslinked by disulphide bridges. Their disulphide bridges are oxidized by iodine in Verhoeff's solution to form ionic sulfonic acid derivatives. These above derivatives are highly basophilic and capable to react with basic dye components of the staining solution.

Reagents

1. Verhoeff's Solution A:

   Haematoxylin – 5 gm

   Absolute alcohol – 100 ml

2. Solution B:

   Ferric chloride – 10 gm

   Distilled water – 100 ml

3. Solution C:

   Iodine – 2 gm

   Potassium iodine – 4 gm

   Distilled water – 100 ml

Working solution

- Add 8 ml of solution B into 20 ml of solution A and to that add 8 ml of solution C.

4. Ferric chloride solution (2%).
5. Acid fuchsin, aqueous solution (1%).
6. Saturated aqueous solution of picric acid.
7. Van Gieson's stain:

   Acid fuchsin, 1% aqueous solution – 5 ml saturated aqueous solution of picric acid – 100 ml.
8. Sodium thiosulphate aqueous solution – 5 gm.

Procedure

1. Deparaffinise and take the section to water.
2. Wash in graded alcohol (absolute, 90%, 80%).
3. Wash in water.
4. Stain in Verhoeff's working solution for 20 minutes.
5. Wash in distilled water.
6. Differentiate in 2% ferric chloride only a few minutes check under the microscope and if differentiate too far restain.
7. Wash in water.
8. Place in 5% sodium thiosulphate for 1 minute.
9. Wash in tap water for 5 minutes.
10. Counterstain in Van Gieson's stain for 1 to 2 minutes.
11. Dehydrate, clear and mount.

Result

Elastic fibres	– Blue to black
Nuclei	– Red
Other tissue elements	– Yellow

3. Staining for Collagen and Collagen Fibres

Masson's Trichrome stain

Principle: This is a connective tissue stain, comparable with the Van Gieson stain, that uses phosphomolybdic and phosphotungstic acids as mordants along with a haematoxylin stain.

Reagent

Solution A

1. Weigerts Iron Haematoxylin solution:

Haematoxylin	– 1 gm
Absolute alcohol	– 100 ml

Solution B

29% Ferric chloride	– 4 ml
Distilled water	– 95 ml
Hydrochloric (conc)	– 1 ml

Mix equal parts of Solution A and Solution B before use.

2. Bierbrich scarlet – acid fuchsin solution:

Bierbrich scarlet, aqueous, 1%	– 90 ml
Acid fushsin, aqueous %	– 10 ml
Glacial acetic acid	– 1 ml

3. Phosphomolybdic – phosphotungstic acid solution:

Phosphomolybdic acid	– 5 gm
Phosphotungstic acid	– 5 gm
Distilled water	– 2.5 gm

4. Aniline blue solution:

Aniline blue	– 2.5 gm
Acetic acid	– 2 ml
Distilled water	– 100 ml

5. 1% Acid alcohol.
6. Light green solution:

Light green	– 5 gm
Distilled water	– 250 ml
Glacial acetic acid	– 2 ml

Heat water, dissolve light green, cool, filter and add acid.

7. Acetic – water (1%) solution:

Glacial acetic acid	– 1 ml
Distilled water	– 100 ml

Procedure

1. Keep the slide in xylene for 10-15 minutes.
2. Wash in graded alcohol (absolute 90%, 80%).
3. Wash in water.
4. Mordant in Bouin's fixative for 1 hr at 56°C.
5. Cool and wash in running tap water until yellow colour disappears.
6. Stain in working iron haematoxylin for 10 minutes.
7. Wash in water.
8. Bierbrich scarlet acid fuchsin solution for 15 minutes and wash in distilled water.
9. Phosphomolybdic acid phosphotungstic acid for 15 minutes.
10. Drain and stain for 5 to 10 minutes in 2.5 per cent aniline blue in 2 per cent acetic acid, or for 1 to 3 minutes in light green solution.
11. Rinse in distilled water.
12. Difference for 3 to 5 minutes in 1 per cent acetic acid solution discards the acid solution.
13. Dehydrate, clear, and mount in Canada balsam.

Result

Nuclei – Black

Muscle, cytoplasm, and keratin – Red

Collagen, mucus – Blue or green.

4. Staining for Fat

Sudan III Fat stain

Principle: The basic principle of this technique is that the dyes are more soluble in fats than in their dye solvents.

Reagents

1. Haematoxylin
2. Sudan III solution:

Sudan III	– 2 gm
70% alcohol	– 50 ml
Acetone	– 50 ml

Procedure

- Dip the section in 70 per cent alcohol only a second.
- Place in Sudan III in a tightly closed container for 5 minutes.
- Wash in 70 per cent alcohol.
    - Wash in water.
- Stain in haematoxylin for 1 minute.
    - Wash in water.
- Differentiate in 1 per cent acid alcohol
    - Wash in water.
- Dip in Lithium Carbonate
    - Wash in water.
- Mount in glycerin jelly.

Results

Fat – Orange to bright red

Nuclei – Blue.

6. *Prussian Blue Reaction for Iron Stain*

Principle: The iron pigments are in the form of ferrichydroxide in tissue. When it is treated with diluted hydrochloric acid, it releases free ferric ion. This ferric ion then reacts with dilute potassium ferrocyanide solution and produces in solution blue compound ferric ferro cyanide.

1. Acidified potassium ferrocyanide solution:

Solution A:

10% hydrochloric acid:

Concentrated HCl	– 10 ml
Distilled water	– 80 ml

Solution B:

Potassium ferrocyanide	– 10 gm
Distilled water	– 100 ml

Mix Equal volume of solution A and solution B before use.

2. Nuclear fast red stain:

Aluminium sulphate	– 5 gm
Nuclear fast red	– 0.1 gm
Distilled water	– 100 ml

Procedure

- Immerse the slides in acidified ferrocyanide solution for 5 to 10 minutes.
- Wash thoroughly with distilled water.
- Counterstain with nuclear fast red for 5 minutes.
- Rinse well with distilled water.
- Dehydrate, clear, and mount on balsam or permount.

Result

Iron Pigment	– Bright blue
Nuclei	– Red
Cytoplasm	– Pink to rose.

REFERENCES

Everson A.G. Pearse, 1996. *Textbook of Histochemistry Theoretical and Applied*, Churchill Livingstone Publication, 3rd edition.

Godkar, P.B. and Godkar, P.D., 2004. *Textbook of Medical Laboratory Technology*, Bhalani Publications, 2nd edition.

John D. Bancroft, 2002. *Theory and Practice of Histological Techniques*, Churchill Livingstone Publication, 5th edition.

Underwood, J.C., 2000. *General and Systemic Pathology*, Churchill Livingstone Publication, 3rd edition.

6

Stool Analysis

Stool is the waste matter discharged from the bowels. Following the digestion and absorption of essential food ingredients in the stomach and intestine, the undigested food and unabsorbed secretions of the stomach, liver, pancreas and intestine appear in the stool.

Appearance

The normal consistency of faeces is described as "Plastic". They are semisolid in appearance in case of normal adults.

Constituents of the Faecal Sample

Faeces consist mainly of cellulose and other undigested foodstuffs, bacteria and water. Other things formed in the stool include desquamated epithelial cells from the gastro intestinal tract and debris of all kinds of bacteria seen in the faecal sample seem to play an important role in Bilirubin metabolism.

Quantity of Sample Excreted in Case of Normal Adult

The kind of food affects the quantity of faecal matter, since vegetable diet increases the amount, while a diet rich in meat decreases the amount of stool formation. The stool also tends to be small and dry on diet high in meat, soft and bulky on a diet high in vegetable and fibre. An adult on average discharges 100 to 300 gms of faecal material per day.

Colour of the Sample

The normal brown colour seen in the sample is due to degradation of bile pigment.

Odour of the Sample

The odour of the sample results from a variety of organic substances. For example indole and skatole are produced by bacteria and also from the degradation of proteins.

Normal Flora Found in the Sample

The faeces of normal individual contains enormous number of various type of bacteria including lactose fermenting and late lactose fermenting coliforms bacilli, Non haemolytic streptococcus, Gram positive bacilli of the acidophillus type and various aerobic and anaerobic spore bearing bacilli.

Collection of the Specimen

(i) The specimen should be collected in sterile clean disposable container.

(ii) The specimen should not be collected in waxy paper, small jars or bottle.

(iii) The specimen should not be contaminated with urine.

(iv) The specimen should be appropriate labelled name of the patient, sex, age for preliminary diagnosis.

(v) The specimen should be examined as quickly as possible. In case of suspective carriers 1 ml sample is sufficient with any abnormal portion. E.g.: containing mucus or pus should be selected.

(vi) In suspected cases of bacillary dysentery, a satisfactory specimen may be obtained by means of a rectal swab and from material collected from the mucus membrane of the rectum.

Clinical Diagnosis of the Sample

Alternation in the colour, odour, consistency and shape may indicate the presence of a disease. Stool is an important specimen for the diagnosis of the diseases of gastro intestinal tract such as diarrhoea, dysentery, parasitic infections, gastro intestinal bleeding, peptic ulcers, carcinoma and malabsorption syndrome including steatorrhoea.

For the detection of bacilli of the enteric and dysenteric groups, suspension of faeces should be shown in a selective liquid/solid medium such as MacConkey, bile salt, lactose agar. The identification of these bacteria depends on their isolation of pure culture and result of fermentation and agglutination test.

In cases of suspected amoebic dysentery, a freshly passed specimens of faeces must be examined. A small fragment of blood stained mucus is placed on a slide and search for motile amoeba which ingest red cells.

Parasites Usually Found in the Faecal Sample

The stool sample is examined for the presence of parasites which include *Entamoeba histolytica, Giardia lamblia, Enterobius vermicularis, Ascaris lumbricoides, Strongyloides* species and *Taenia* species.

6.1 Gross Examination of the Stool

Aim: To perform the gross examination and physical examination of the given stool sample.

Gross examination: The given stool sample was observed for the following:

(a) Consistency and forms: The normal consistency of the faeces is described as "PLASTIC" well formed stool.

Consistency of Abnormal Stool

Sl. No.	Abnormal consistency	Expected reasons
1.	Pale, bulky, frothy	Steatorrhoea
2.	Hard	Constipation
3.	Flattened and ribbon like	Obstruction in the bowel of human
4.	Semi solid condition	Mild diarrhoea after taking laxative, digestive upset
5.	Watery condition	Bacterial infection, purgative
6.	Rice water stool	Cholera
7.	Voluminous watery stool	Cholera, food poisoning
8.	Fresh blood and mucus	Dysentery
9.	Pasty	Obstructive jaundice, alcoholic
10.	Loose	Inflammatory bowel bacillary Dysentery, Typhoid Amoebiasis carcinoma.

(b) Colour: A normal faeces is light or dark brown in colour due to the presence of bile pigments. The colour of the stool may change with the kind of food intake.

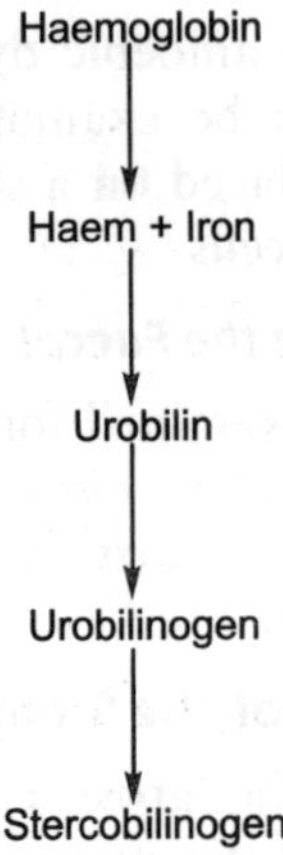

Abnormal Colour

Sl. No.	Abnormal colour	Possible reasons
1.	Black	Bleeding in the upper gastro intestinal tract, iron administration in iron deficiency anaemia
2.	Bright red	Gastro intestinal tract, Bleeding piles, contamination with menstrual blood
3.	Clay coloured	Post hepatic jaundice, obstruction the flow of bile to the intestine
4.	White	After barium meal
5.	Dark brown	Haemolytic anaemia, diet high in meat prolonged exposure to air
6.	Grey	Chocolate and coco ingestion
7.	Grey silvery	Steatorrihoea
8.	Greyish white	Barium ingestion, biliary tract obstruction
9.	Very pale gray	Diet high in milk products
10.	Green or Yellowish green	Ingestion of laxatives of vegetable origin

(c) Odour: The characteristic odour of faeces is due bacterial action on protein and other residues that produce substance such as Indole, Skatole, Phenol, Hydrogen sulphide and ammonia.

Abnormal Odour: Extremely food, putrid, sour or rancid smell may indicate a possible different clinical condition from the presence of malignout tumor to indigestion and formation of acidity.

(d) Casts: Casts of the bowels are occasionally found. They are passed in shreds or in the form of a complete cast of the intestine. This condition is termed as Enteritis membrane or colica mucosa. These casts are more commonly found in women than in men and it occurs due to impairment of general nutrition and spastic condition.

Fibrin: It is difficult to identify fibrin in the stools and hence autopsy findings of fibrin are common in dysenteric patients but in these cases fibrin is attached to the wall of the intestine. It is logical to assume that it is last off and appears in the stool. Fibrin masses are found especially in membrane colitis.

Tissue remnants: Tissue remnants emanate either from tumor of the intestinal wall or from necrotic mucous membrane changes. Very small necrotic masses have been seen in the stools of patients with typhoid fever in the second week or third week.

Other organic material: Other organic material may be parasites or various calculi. Among calculi are gall stones that are identified by their smooth and facetted surface and their light weight small stones are so easily broken up that they are no longer recognizable when they reach the lower end of the stool.

Microscopic Findings

(a) Epithelia cells: Epithelia cells from all portion of the tract are likely to find their way into the blood. There may be pure unchanged stratified squamous epithelia cells from the region of the ances, pure types of squamous cells are rubbed off unchanged from the anal orifice by passage of the stool. Cylindrical cells from points higher up are seem as slightly distorted cells, found in stools of typhoid, diarrhoea of children. They may appear singly or grouped as they are in the intestinal wall. These cells are sometimes swollen with fat droplets.

(b) Leucocytes: They are not commonly found in the faeces. They are abundant naturally when there is pus formation as in ulcerative conditions in the tract—Eosinophilic granules may be seen. Leucocytes that are large enough to be designated giant cells have been seen in faeces. The presence of a few leucocytes in conjunction with epithelial cells in infantile stools indicates an irritation process.

(c) Pus cells: Macroscopically the grayish masses that microscopically prove to be collections of pus cells may be observed. Pus coming from a higher point in the small intestine would undergo changes before being expelled in the stool mass. The presence of much pus always indicates an ulcerative pathology.

(d) Erythrocytes: The findings of red cells in faeces usually indicates ulceration. Exceptionally they are found in venous stagnation. Well preserved corpuscles are seen in cases of haemorrhage from stacis low down (haemorrhoids) vein bleeding.

(e) Detritus: Besides the various elements already described there are found in stools some microscopic particles that are extremely small and impossible to identify. This material is termed as detritus. It includes intimately digested muscle remnants, plant cells, bacteria, epithelia and presence of large quantity of detritus is a good indication of the chemical and mechanical efficiency of gastro intestinal digestion.

(f) Crystals: Many crystals are formed in faeces, some derived from food, other from the chemical change in the intestine.

Triple phosphate or ammonium magnesium phosphate crystals: These are the commonest one usually found. They vary in size and best developed crystals are seen in fluid stools. Their shape is that of the knife rest or coffin lid, but some are more or less irregular. Triple phosphates are never bile stained. They are insoluble in ammonium carbonate solution that distinguishes them from the neutral phosphate crystals that they closely resemble.

D1-Calcium phosphate or neutral phosphate of lime crystals: These appear in the form and size of those found in urine, large on smaller shears with the point lying together. They are occasionally bile stained and they occur as rosette. They are freely soluble in acids and are found in normal stools, particularly when alkaline stools have been allowed to stand for sometime.

Neutral magnesium phosphate or trimagnesium phosphate crystals: They are found in stools showing ammonia decomposition. They occur as irregular shears. They are soluble in acetic acid and become opaque when ammonium carbonate solution is added.

Calcium carbonate crystals: They appear as round or dumbell shaped crystals or amorphous granules. The addition of acetic or other mineral acid dissolves them with gas formation, sulphuric acid causes them to assume a sheaf like form. These crystals are commonly seen in the stool of milk fed children.

Calcium oxalate crystals: They are found in ingested vegetables such as tomatoes, spinach. They are not seen on a milk or meat diet. They appear in various forms in faeces as envelope shape, as typical rosette and as rhomboid varieties. They are insoluble in acetic acid and alkalis but are soluble in mineral acids.

Crystals from sediments: Dark bismuth crystals are found after ingestion of bismuth sub nitrate and after the intake of substances with iron, charcoal and manganese pass as black amorphous granules.

Cholesterol: They appear as flat superimposed plates and are easily soluble in hot alcohol and chloroform. They appear particularly in children where large amount of mucus is passed. It is commonly seen in meconium.

Charcol leyden crystals: They appear as they do in sputum as colourless octahedral with sharp margins and generally broken angles. They are commonly seen embedded in mucus. These crystals are abundant in cases of helminthiasis.

Hemin crystals: They are seen in faeces only after ingestion of food sausage, but heamatoidin crystals are common. They occur as reddish yellow shombic plates, columnus needles or bundles of needles.

Bilirubin: They appear as haematoidin as rhombic needle shaped crystals and is found in infantile stools.

Uric acid and uric acid salts: They are found except as the result of contamination with urine.

6.2 Test for Lactose as a Reducing Substance

Aim: To test the presence of lactose in the given fecal sample by benedict's test.

Principle: Reducing sugar like glucose contains an aldehyde group called as aldolase that reduces the blue coloured alkaline cupric sulphate to yellow red cuprous oxide. When benedict's quantitative reagent 5 ml is heated with 8 drops of emulsified fecal sample. 0.5 ml lactose present in the sample reduces the cupric iron present in the reagent to cuprous ions. Alkaline medium is provided by sodium carbonate present in the reagent. The original colour of benedict's reagent is blue and changes to green, yellow, orange or red according to the concentration of lactose present in the fecal sample.

Materials Required

(a) Fecal sample

(b) Physiological saline

(c) Benedict's solution

Preparation of reagent:

Sodium citrate	– 173 gm
Sodium carbonate	– 100 gm
Crystalline copper sulphate	– 17.3 gm

Sodium citrate and sodium carbonate was weighed and dissolved in about 900 ml of dissolved water it was boiled for 2–3 minutes and cooled and about 17.3 gm of copper sulphate was weighed and added and dissolves to make 1 litre. The reagent is stored in polythene container and is stable at room temperature.

(d) Standard glasswares.

Procedure

1. Two test tubes were taken one for test and the other for control.
2. To the test tube, small amount of the fecal sample is added. To the control tube distilled water is added.
3. To both the tubes 5 ml of Benedict's reagent is added. The tubes was mixed well and placed in boiling water bath for 5 minutes.
4. The tubes were cooled in room temperature in cold water bath. A positive reaction depends on the presence of yellow, orange or brick red precipitate.

Observation: The above procedure was done for the given fecal sample after boiling it for 5 minutes and then cool to room temperature. Development of brick red precipitate was observed which indicates the presence of reducing sugar like glucose and lactose.

Result: The given sample contains reducing sugar like lactose.

Caution: Some non sugars like uric acid, creatinine, ascorbic acid have a similar reducing property and hence may answer for the positive result.

Clinical significance: Lactase is an enzyme which breaks lactose to glucose and galactose.

- If lactase is deficient in the gut lactose is not digested or absorbed but ferments to lactic acid with the production of the gas.
- This causes abdominal pain and diarrhoea which may be persistent and severe. Especially in young children when there is lactase deficiency, fecal specimen usually contains lactose and has low pH due to the presence of lactic acid.

6.3 Test for Occult Blood

Aim: To test for occult blood in the given faecal sample.

Principle: The term occult means "Hidden". The test is capable of detecting even minute amount of blood which is not visible for naked eye in the given faecal sample. These procedures actually detect free haemoglobin from lysed red cells. The test is based on peroxidase like activity of haemoglobin and myoglobin which catalyses the oxidation of an indicator such as 3, 3^1, 5, 5^1–tetra methyl benzidene by an organic peroxidase such as cumene hydro peroxidase. The colour change is from orange to green to dark blue. The peroxidase activity of haemoglobin decomposes hydrogen peroxide and liberated active oxygen oxidases, the organic compound benzidene.

Materials Required

Preparation of reagents

- Saturated solution of benzidene in glacial acetic acid (4 gm to 100 ml).
- Hydrogen peroxidase (3% in distilled H_2O).

Procedure

1. Mix equal parts of A and B solution in a test tube just before use.
2. Add a pinch of motion sample.
3. The appearance of green or blue colour within 5 minutes indicates the presence of blood.

Result may be graded as follows:

Pale blue	-	Positive
Dark blue	-	Strongly positive
Blue black	-	Positive
No colour change	-	Negative

Result: The dark blue colour change indicates that the given sample is strongly positive.

Clinical significance: Presence of blood in the stool indicates gastrointestinal bleeding. Red blood cells may not be visible in case of slow bleeding and if the bleeding is high up in the gut region blood is half digested and the stool looks black without the presence of RBC. It is called malena.

- If the RBC are seen in the stool the bleeding has occurred in the large intestine.
- The finding of occult blood may establish whether an ulcer in the digestive tract is bleeding. The smallest amount of meat in the diet is likely to give a positive benzidene reaction, hence the patient must be kept on a meat free diet for atleast 3 days before taking up the test.
- A positive reaction means bleeding from any position of the tract. Blood may be found either in benign or malignant disease.
- Blood is encountered in melena (black tarry stool), haemorrhagic enteritis, from fissures, polyps, rectal papilloma and typhoid perforations.
- Duodenal ulcers may lead to bleeding.

6.4 Test for Fat

Aim: To demonstrate the presence of fat in the stool.

Principle: The fat-soluble dye (Sudan II, Sudan IV oil Red – 0) differentiates fat globules from other materials in the stool. Fat is normally present in stool to some extent.

Materials Required

- Ethanol – 95%

- Saturated Ethanolic **Solution** of Sudan III
- Glacial acetic acid – 36% (v/v).

Procedure

1. A small amount of thoroughly mixed stool sample is placed on a glass slide.
2. Two to three drops of water are added to the stool and is mixed thoroughly. Two to three drops of ethanol (95%) is added followed by the addition of two drops of ethanolic solution of Sudan III.
3. This is mixed well and coverslipped. The coverslip is applied by wet mounting technique and the set up is allowed to stand for 5 minutes.
4. The slide may be put in a petridish with a wet blotting paper at the bottom to present drying. The slide is examined under high power objective.

Observation: Yellow orange or red refractive droplets of fat globules will be seen at the collected edge of coverslip. This is called as neutral fat. Fat substances are frequently found in the stool as neutral fat, free fatty acids are soaps.

Neutral fat

- Neutral fat appear in droplets or in scales of irregular forms. The fat scales are usually unstained.
- The fat droplets appear round and are often stained yellow. In stools of infants, fat appear just as the dust in the microscopic picture of a milk.

Fatty acids

- Fatty acids appear as drops or scales and are difficult to distinguish from neutral fat at time showing characteristics crystals.
- The crystals appear as fine needles with pointed ends similar forms seen in sputum.
- They also appear as lancet shaped plates occasionally seen in infantile stools or as needles that resemble soaps.

Soaps: Soaps appear as scales or crystals. They appear lesser than neutral fats or fatty acids and they may be unstained or slightly stained. They may appear yellow due to stercobilin or bilirubin. They usually appear as unstained needles but one variety that can be found is seeing with fire radial striations.

Result: The given sample shows the presence of, neutral fats, fatty acid and soapy fats.

Clinical significance: In the normal dried stools of infants the fat should not exceed 20% marked increase is always a biliary or a pancreatic defect.

- Pancreatic juice has the principle function in the digestion of fat.
- Wohlgemuth states that the lipase of the pancreatic fluid exists in a inactive form and it is activated by the bile. The bile also helps to dissolve free fatty acid formed by the action of the pancreatic lipase on neutral fats, for these acids are insoluble in water but they are mildly soluble in bile. Hence bile assists in the absorption of fat.
- Infantile stools show a great deal of fat as neutral fats, fatty acids and soaps. Adults' stools show fat but usually only soaps are seen. They are not found in healthy person after a test meal. Naked eye appearance of fat means increased fat content. Fatty diarrhea is called Steatorrhoea. Seventy-six grams of fat/day is seen in malabsorption syndrome, chronic pancreatitis and obstructive jaundice.

6.5 Direct Saline Faecal Smear

Aim: To observe the presence of helminth eggs, amoeba, trophozoites, under low power magnification using direct saline faecal smear method.

Principle: Helminth eggs can be detected and usually identified under low power magnification. Amoeba, trophozoites and cyst can be detected but they must be stained for positive identification (exception, *E. histolytica* cyst containing chromatid bars or trophozoites containing red blood cells). The trophozoites of flagellates can be identified by characteristic appearance and locomotion. Vital stains are suitable temporary preparation whereas permanent smear may be stained with haematoxylin or trichrome. The permanent stains give better results than temporary stain preparation. Care is taken to see that during the smear preparation, one should avoid the clumping of faecal material under the cover glass. It is essential to employ both saline and iodine stained smear on a faecal slide, since they supplement each other.

Material Required

- Physiological saline, cover glass, tissue paper.
- Faecal sample and other standard lab wares.

Procedure

- One or two drops of physiological saline is placed on a slide with an help of an applicator stick 1 to 2 ml of faecal sample is taken.
- It is essential to avoid non faecal elements unless schistosomal eggs or amoeba is suspected in which cases, flecks of mucus and blood is selected. The mixture is stirred well and is made into a homogenous suspension.
- It is essential to remove coarse fibers, seeds, sand, etc., It is then covered with a coverslip and is observed under the microscope.

Observation

A satisfactory smear contains a maximum of observable faecal elements without any objects of protozoan size (8 to 30 mm) being obscured. In many laboratories it is customary to prepare a saline faecal smear on one end of the slide and a iodine stained faecal smear on the other end of the same slide to aid in identification of protozoan cyst.

Result: The given faecal contains eggs of *Ascaris lumbricoides*.

6.6 Formol Ether Concentration Technique

Aim: To perform formol ether concentration technique for the identification of cyst, oocyst and larva.

Principle: In the (Ridley and Hagwood 1956) modified method faeces are emulsified in formol water. The suspension is strained to remove large faecal particles. Ether or Ethyl acetate is added and the mixed suspension is centrifuged. Cyst and oocyst larvae and eggs are fixed and sedimented and the faecal debris is separated in a layer between the ether and the formol water. Faecal fat is dissolved in the ether. This technique is used to concentrate a wide range of faecal parasites from fresh or preserved faeces. Risk of the laboratory-acquired infection from the faecal pathogen is minimized because organisms are killed by the formalin solution when concentrating the oocyst of coxedia and additional centrifugation stage is required (formal ether oocyst concentration technique).

Materials Required

- Formol water – 10% v/v.
- Diethyl ether or ethyl acetate side (size of the hole = 400 – 450 mm).
- Faecal sample, centrifuge, centrifuge tubes.
- Other standard Lab wares.

Preparation of formol water 10% v/v: 500 ml of strong formaldehyde solution is mixed well with 450 ml of distilled water.

Procedure: A stick or a rod is used to emulsify 1 gm of faeces about the size of a peanut in about 4 ml of 10% formol water contained in a screw capped bottle or tube. A further 3 to 4 ml of 10% v/v formol water is added and the bottle is capped and mixed well by shaking the condense in the bottle. The emulsified faeces is sieved, suspension is collected in a beaker. The suspension is transferred to a conical centrifuge tube and 3 to 4 ml of diethyl ether or ethyl acetate is added to it. The centrifuge tube is stoppered and mixed for 1 minute, if using a portex mixture the tube is left unstoppered and mixed well for 15 seconds. A tissue or a piece of cloth is rapped around the top of the tube and the stopper is loosened because considerable pressure will have built up inside the tube. It is centrifuged immediately at 3000 rpm for 1 minute. After centrifuging the parasite will have sedimented to the bottom of the tube and faecal debris will have collected in a layer between the ether and the formol water. With the help of stick the layer of the faecal debris is loosened and allowed to flow out from the side of the tube. The tube is invested to discard the ether faecal debris and formol water. The sediment will remain. The tube is returned to its upright position and the fluid is allowed to flow from the side of the tube to drain to the bottom. The bottom of the tube is tapped and to resuspend and to mix the sediment. The sediment is transferred to a slide and is covered with a cover glass.

Preparation is examined microscopically using 10x objective with the condenser closed sufficiently to give good contrast. The 40x objective is used to examine the small cyst and eggs. To access in the identification of cyst, a small drop of iodine is allowed to seen around the cover glass.

Result: The given faecal sample contains eggs of to *Taenia solium*, eggs of *Enterobius vermicularis*.

6.7 Floatation Technique

(Zinc Sulphate Floatation Technique)

Aim: To determine zinc sulphate floatation technique in the given faecal sample.

Principle: A zinc sulphate solution is used which has a specific gravity of 1.800 – 1.200 faeces are emulsified in the solution and left undisturbed for the eggs and cysts to float on the surface when they are covered with the glass zinc sulphate technique is recommended for concentrating the cyst of *Giardia lambdia* and *E. histolytica* other nematode eggs are concentrated less well.

Materials Required

Zinc sulphate solution 33% w/v

Specific gravity 1.800 – 1.200

Preparation of Zinc Sulphate

Zinc sulphate – 165 gm

Distilled water – 500 ml

The salt zinc sulphate is weighed and transferred into a leak proof bottle of about one litre capacity. The amount of water is measured and added to the chemical the bottle is stoppered and mixed well. The bottle is allowed to stand in a contains of hot water to dissolve the zinc sulphate. The solution is allowed to cool under room temperature using a hydrometer the relative density of the solution is checked if the density is not within the 1.180 – 1.200 add more chemical or water to bring the solution within the correct density range. The bottle is labeled and stored at room temperature.

Procedure: Fill the tube at least one quarter full with the zinc sulphate solution and on estimated amount of 1 gm of faeces using a rod or stick emulsify the specimen in the solution fill the tube with the zinc sulphate solution and mix well strain the faecal suspension to remove large faecal particles return the suspension to the tube. The tube is allowed to stand in a complete vertical position in a rack. Using a plastic bulb pipette or pasteur pipette further solution is added to ensure that the tube is filled to the brim carefully place a completely clean cover glass on top of the tube, trapping of air bubbles as avoided. The setup is left undisturbed for 30-45 minutes to give time for the cyst and eggs to float the cover glass is carefully lifted from the tube and is placed downwards on a slide it is essential to avoid contamination with the fingers during the preparation process. It is microscopically examined using 10x and 40x objective and a drop of iodine is added the cover glass to identify the cyst.

Observation: In the satisfactory faecal smear, eggs of *Entamoeba histolytica, Giardia lamblia,* Hookworm, and eggs of *Schistosoma haematobium* were observed.

Result: The given faecal sample contains *E. histolytica, Giardia lamblia*, Hookworm, and *Schistosoma haematobium.*

REFERENCES

Geo F. Brooks, Janet S. Butel, Stephen A. Morse, 2002. *Medical Microbiology*, Tata McGraw Hill Publication.

John Bernard Henry, 2001. *Clinical Diagnosis and Management by Laboratory Methods*. W.B. Saunders Publication, 20th edition.

Kanai L. Mukherjee, 2002. *Medical Laboratory Technology—A procedure manual for routine diagnostic tests*, Tata McGraw Hill Publishing, 11th edition.

Manual of Basic Techniques for a Health Laboratory, World Health Organization, III edition, New Age International Publishers, 2005.

Monica Cheesbrough, 1998. *District Laboratory Practice in Tropical Countries*, Part I, Cambridge University Press.

Patrick R. Murray, Ellen Jo Baron, James H. Jorgensen, Michael A. Pfaller, Robert H. Yoken, 2003. *Manual of Clinical Microbiology*. Vol. 1, VIII edition. ASM Press Washington DC.

Praful B. Godkar and Darshan P. Godkar, 2003. *Textbook of Medical Technology*, III edition, Bhalani Publications.

Ramnik Sood, 2002. *Medical Laboratory Technology—Methods and Interpretation*, Brother Publications, V edition, 2002.

7

Urine Analysis

Urine is a clear, amber-coloured fluid formed by the kidneys that carries metabolic wastes out of the body. As the blood circulates, it collects excretory products from the tissues and these substances are separated from the blood by the kidneys and eliminated chiefly in the urine. The urine is then stored in the bladder and passes out of the body via the urethra. The amount passed depends on fluid intake and other factors. Urine has 95 per cent water, in which are dissolved urea, uric acid, creatinine, and other waste products. Normal urine also contains small amounts of substances such as sodium, potassium, and calcium; these substances are excreted by the kidneys when excessive amounts are present in the bloodstream.

Routine urine analysis is mainly performed for two purposes:

(1) To find out metabolic or endocrine disorders of the body.

(2) To detect intrinsic conditions that may adversely affect the urinary tract or the kidneys.

Normal Values in Urine Analysis

General characteristics	Chemical determinations	Microscopic examination
Colour: Pale yellow	Glucose: Negative	Casts: Negative Occasional Hyaline casts
Appearance: Clear	Ketone: Negative	RBC: Negative or rare

(Contd...)

Specific gravity: 1.003-1.030	Blood: Negative	WBC: Negative or rare
pH: 4.7 – 7.5	Protein : Negative	Crystals: Negative
Volume: 1200 ml/24 h	Bilirubin: Negative	Epithelial cells: Few
	Urobilinogen: 0.5 – 4.0 mg/dl	
	Nitrate: Negative	

7.1 Physical Examination of Urine

Aim: To perform physical examination of the given urine sample.

Requirements: Pasteur pipettes, pH paper, urinometer, measuring cylinder.

Procedure: Colour, appearance and odour of the urine sample is noted. Volume is measured using the measuring cylinder. A drop of urine is placed on the pH paper and the colour change is noted. To determine the specific gravity the container is filled three fourth with urine and the urinometer is allowed to float taking care that it does not touch the sides of the container. The reading is noted from the scale.

Clinical implications

Urine volume:

- Polyuria

  Diabetic ketoacidosis

  Partial obstruction of urinary tract
- Oliguria

  Dehydration

  Renal disease
- Anuria

  Complete urinary tract obstruction

  Glomerulonephritis

Urine specific gravity

- Hyposthenuria

  Diabetes insipidus

  Glomerulonephritis

- Hypersthenuria

  Diabetes mellitus

  Nephrosis

  Dehydration

Urine appearance

- Pathologic urine is cloudy; it may be due to urinary tract infections or may be because of the presence of RBCs, WBCs, epithelial cells or bacteria.

Urine colour

- Colourless

  Large fluid intake

  Chronic interstitial nephritis

  Untreated diabetes mellitus

  Diabetes insipidus

  Nervousness

- Orange colour

  Fever

  Bilirubin

  Ingestion of carrot or vitamin A

  Medications like phenazopyridine, nitrofurantoin

- Green

  Pseudomonal infection

- Pink to red

  RBCs

  Haemoglobin, methemoglobin

- Brown to black urine
  - Homogentisic acid
  - Melanin
  - Phenol poisoning

Urine odour

- The urine of patients with diabetes mellitus may have a fruity odour.
- UTI results in foul smelling urine.
- Urine of infants with inherited disorder of amino acid metabolism smelling like maple or burned sugar.
- Phenylketonuria, mousy smell may be evident.

Urine pH

- Acidic urine
  - Metabolic acidosis
  - Diabetic ketosis
  - Diarrhea
  - Renal tuberculosis
- Alkaline urine
  - UTI
  - Metabolic acidosis
  - Respiratory alkalosis

7.2 Determination of Glucose

(Benedict's Qualitative Test)

Aim: To determine the presence of glucose in the given Urine sample.

Principle: Glucose contains an aldehyde group that reduces the blue colour alkaline cupric sulphate to yellow colour cuprous oxide. Under special circumstance reducing substances other than glucose may give false positive results and the specimen should be re-tested for true glucose with the help of test strips.

Requirements: Urine sample, Benedict's reagent, standard glasswares.

Procedure: To five ml of Benedict's reagent 0.5 ml of centrifuged urine sample is added. The test tube is placed in a boiling water bath for 5 minutes. It is cooled and the solution and precipitate are observed for colour change and the result is graded as follows:

Colour	Sugar Concentration
Blue	Nil
Green, no precipitate	Trace
Green with precipitate	1+
Brown and cloudy	2+
Orange and cloudy	3+
Red and cloudy	4+

Clinical significance

Increased Glucose occurs in:

- Diabetes mellitus
- Endocrine disorders
- Liver and pancreatic disease
- Pregnancy with gestational diabetes
- Renal glycosuria.

7.3 Microscopic Examination of Urine Sediment

Aim: To perform microscopic examination of the given urine sample.

Requirements: Urine sample, standard glasswares.

Procedure: The urine sample is centrifuged at 2500 rpm for 5 minutes. The supernatant is discarded and one drop of the deposit is taken in a glass slide and cover slipped. The sediment is observed under high power objective. The various findings observed in the sediment may be as follows:

Pus cells: These are round cells that contain granules. Normal urine may contain 3-4 pus cells/HPF.

Red cells: These are smaller and more refractile than white cells. They have definite nuclei and contain no granules.

Casts: The following casts can be found in urine:

- Hyaline casts, which are colourless and empty.
- Waxy casts, which are hyaline casts that have remained in the tubules for a long time. They are thicker and denser than hyaline casts, often appear intended or twisted, and may be yellow in colour.
- Cellular casts, which contain white cells or red cells.
- Granular casts, which contain irregular sized granules.

Epithelial cells: They are nucleated and vary in size and shape.

Crystals: These have a characteristic refractile appearance:

- Uric acid crystal, these appear in diamond rhombic or rosette form. These are usually stained with urinary pigments as yellow or red brown.
- Calcium oxalate crystals, these are colourless and octahedral or envelope shaped.
- Cystine crystals, these are colourless, refractile, hexagonal plates with equal or unequal sides.
- Tyrosine crystals, these appear in the form of fine refractile needles occurring in clusters or sheaves.
- Leucine crystals, these are oily highly refractile spheroids with radial and concentric striations.
- Cholesterol crystals, these are large, flat and transparent with notched corners.
- Triple phosphates, they are colourless prisms with three to six sides and frequently with oblique end.

Clinical Significance

Cells

- Leucocytes: > 5 cells per HPF is seen in UTI, Glomerular nephritis, Dehydration, Pyelonephritis.
- Erythrocytes: Indicates bleeding in the urinary tract or Glomerulo nephritis.

- Epithelial cells: > 5 cells per HPF is seen in tubular damage, pyelonephritis and kidney transplant rejection.

Casts

Present in Glomerular damage, renal inflammation and renal infection:

- Hyaline cast: Seen in even the mildest kind of renal disease.
- Red cell cast: Glomerulonephritis and bacterial endocarditis.
- White cell cast: Renal infection, Nephritis, Glomerular disease.
- Granular cast: Significant renal disease.
- Waxy cast: Severe chronic renal failure, tubular inflammation.
- Fatty cast: Nephrotic syndrome, chronic glomerulonephritis.

Crystals

- Uric acid crystal: Gout, chronic nephritis, acute febrile conditions.
- Calcium oxalate crystal: Oxalate calculi, diabetes mellitus, liver diseases.
- Cystine crystals: Congenital cystinuria. They can form calculi.
- Tyrosine: Severe liver disease and tyrosinosis.
- Leucine: Severe hepatitis, maple syrup urine disease.
- Cholesterol: Nephritis, Chyluria, Excessive tissue breakdown.
- Triple phosphates: Chronic cystitis, chronic pyelitis, enlarged prostate.

7.4 Test for Proteins—Sulphosalicylic Acid Method

Aim: To test the presence of protein in the given sample by sulphosalicylic acid test method.

Principle: Sulphosalicylic acid is an anion precipitant that works by the neutralization of the protein cation which leads to the precipitation of the proteins.

Requirements: Urine sample, 3 per cent sulphosalicylic acid, standard glasswares.

Procedure: Two ml of centrifuged urine is taken in a test tube and equal volume of sulphosalicylic acid reagent is added. It is mixed well and allowed to stand for 10 minutes. The degree of turbidity is noted and the results are graded as follows:

No turbidity or no increase in turbidity	:	Trace
Distinct turbidity but no granulation	:	1+
Turbidity with granulation but no flocculation	:	2+
Turbidity with granulation and flocculation	:	3+
Clumps of precipitate	:	4+

Normal value: Nil or Trace.

Clinical significance: The presence of increased amounts of protein in the urine can be an important indicator of renal disease. However, there are other physiological conditions (e.g. exercise, fever) that can lead to increase protein excretion in urine. Proteinuria occurs by two main mechanisms: damage to the glomerulus or defect in the re-absorption process that occurs in the tubules.

- Glomerular damage
  - Glomerulonephritis
  - Diabetes mellitus
  - Nephrotic syndrome
- Diminished tubular reabsorption
  - Renal tubular disease
  - Pyelonephritis

Proteinuria can occur in non-renal diseases (functional proteinuria) like leukemia, haematologic disorder, septicemia, hyperthyroidism.

Postural proteinuria results from the excretion of protein by some patients when they stand or move about. This type of proteinuria is intermittent and disappears when the patient lies down.

7.5 Test for Ketone Bodies—Nitroprusside Test Method

Aim: To test the presence of ketones in the given urine sample.

Principle: Nitroprusside reacts with ketone bodies such as acetone and acetoacetic acid in the presence of alkali such as ammonium hydroxide and results in the formation of a pink colour ring.

Requirements: Urine sample, Rothera's mixture, Ammonia solution, Standard glasswares.

Procedure: A small amount of Rothera's mixture is taken in a dry test tube. Three to four drops of centrifuged urine is added so as to moisten the powder at the bottom of the tube. It is layered with 1-2 ml of ammonia solution. Presence of acetone or acetoacetate is detected by the formation of pink to violet colour ring and the results are graded as follows:

No colour change	:	Negative
Slight pink colour ring	:	Trace
Deep pink colour ring	:	2+ to 3+
Rapid forming deep purple ring	:	4+

Normal value: Negative.

Clinical significance: In healthy persons ketones are formed in the liver and are completely metabolized so that only negligible amounts appear in the urine. However, when carbohydrate metabolism is altered an excess amount of ketones is formed because fat becomes the predominant body fuel instead of carbohydrates.

Ketosis and ketonuria can occur in the following situations:

- Metabolic conditions
    - Diabetes mellitus
    - Renal glycosuria
    - Glycogen storage disease

- Dietary conditions
  - Starvation, fasting
  - High fat diets
  - Prolonged vomiting, diarrhoea
  - Low carbohydrate diet.

7.6 Determination of Bile Pigment

Aim: To test the presence of Bile pigment in the given sample.

Principle: When Barium chloride is added to urine it combines with sulphate radicals in the urine and precipitates of Barium sulphate is formed. Bilirubin present in the urine adheres to barium sulphate. Ferric chloride present in Fouchet's reagent oxidizes yellow bilirubin to green biliverdin.

Requirements: Urine sample, Fouchet's reagent, standard glasswares.

Procedure: The pH of the urine is checked and if alkaline it is made acidic by adding acetic acid. Three to four ml of urine is taken in a centrifuge tube and equal amount of 10 per cent barium chloride is added. It is centrifuged at 2500 rpm for 5 minutes. Two drops of Fouchet's reagent is added to the sediment. The change of colour to green indicates the presence of bilirubin.

Clinical Implications

Increased Bilirubin occurs in:

- Hepatitis—Acute or chronic
- Obstructive biliary tract disease
- Liver or biliary tract tumors
- Septicemia.

7.7 Determination of Urobilinogen

(Wallace-Diamond quick screen method)

Aim: To test the presence of Urobilinogen in the given Urine sample.

Principle: Ehrlich's reagent reacts with Urobilinogen and imparts a pink colour. Porphobilinogen also gives a red colour with Ehrlich's reagent. This is differentiated by the addition of sodium acetate, which alters the pH and intensifies the colour given by Urobilinogen but not by Porphobilinogen.

Requirements: Urine sample, Ehrlich's reagent, sodium acetate, standard glasswares.

Procedure: Screening Step: One ml of Ehrlich's reagent is added to 4 ml of fresh urine sample and is gently warmed. A pink colour appears in case of positive reaction and if positive confirmatory test is done.

Confirmatory Test: Two ml of urine sample is mixed with 2 ml of Ehrlich's reagent. The immediate appearance of red colour at this stage is suggestive of porphobilinogen. For confirmation, 4 ml of sodium acetate is added and mixed well. If the colour persists it indicates urobilinogen. If the colour fades it is probably porphobilinogen.

Clinical significance: Urine urobilinogen is increased when there is increased destruction to tissues, pulmonary infarction and excessive bruising, hepatic damage, biliary disease, cirrhosis and acute hepatitis.

7.8 Determination of Bile Salts

Aim: To test the presence of bile salts in the given urine sample.

Principle: Bile salts when present in urine lowers the surface tension of urine. When sulphur powder is added on the surface of urine, sulphur particles sink to the bottom of the tube.

Requirements: Urine sample, sulphur powder, standard glasswares.

Procedure: Three to four ml of urine is taken in a test tube. Dry sulphur powder is sprinkled on the surface of the urine sample. If sulphur powder sinks to the bottom of the tube it shows the presence of bile salts.

Clinical Significance

- Liver diseases.
- Ca-Gall bladder and bile duct.

REFERENCES

Arthur C. Gyton, John E. Hall, 2006. *Textbook of Medical Physiology*, Saunders Publications, 11th edition.

Gerard J. Tortora, Bryan Derrickson, 2006. *Principles of Anatomy and Physiology*, John Wiley and Sons ICL, 11th edition.

J. Ochei, A. Kolhatkar, 2000. *Medical Laboratory Science—Theory* and *Practice*, Tata McGraw Hill.

Praful B. Godkar, Darshan P. Godkar, 2004. *Textbook of Medical Laboratory Technology*, Bhalani Publications, 2nd edition.

Vincent Marks, Thomas Cantor, Dusan Mesko, Rudolf Pullman, Gabriela Nosalova, 2003. *Differential Diagnosis in Laboratory Medicine*, Springer Publication.

8

Sputum Analysis

8.1 Sputum Collection

Specimen: Early morning specimen or the entire 24 hours specimen.

Container: Sterile wide mouthed disposable container with screw cap (50-60 ml capacity).

Instructions Given to Patient

- The mouth should be rinsed well by using water.
- The sputum must be coughed up from the lungs or bronchi and placed carefully in the container.

Procedure for Sputum Sampling

1. Remember that sputum specimens must come from the bronchi. Postnasal secretions or saliva is unacceptable. Expectoration; ultrasonic nebulization, chest physiotherapy, nasotracheal or tracheal suctioning and bronchoscopy are various methods used to obtain sputum and bronchial specimens. Early morning specimens are the best.
2. Instruct the patients (if possible) to remove dentures, rinse the mouth with water and gargle.
3. The patient should first clear the nose and throat, take three or four deep breaths, perform a series of short coughs, and then inhale deeply and cough forcefully to raise a sputum specimen.
4. The sputum should be expectorated into a sterile container with the proper preservative if indicated.

Two to three ml sample is adequate. Place the sealed container into a leak proof biohazard bag and transfer it to laboratory after labelling properly.

5. Sputum specimens are usually not refrigerated and should be taken to the laboratory as soon as possible. Include the pertinent information, such as type of specimen, appearance, preservative, tests ordered, date and time of collection and deposition of specimen.
6. Document the specimen appearance and the patient's response to the procedure.

Interventions

Sputum sampling

(a) Pre-test patient preparation:
- Explain purpose and procedure of sputum specimen collection. An early morning specimen produces the best organism-concentrated sputum sample of deeply located pulmonary secretions.
- Obtain a sputum collection kit and supplies. Instruct the patients about all aspects of collections, including any specific body positioned or chest physiotherapy, such as chest clapping.
- Inform the patient not to touch inside of the container.

(b) Post-patient care:
- Evaluate patient's outcomes and counsel appropriately about treatment and self-care for respiratory illness.
- Monitor the respiratory status as necessary and intervene appropriately when indicated.

Transportation of sputum specimen

If the laboratory is located at a distance from the site of specimen collection, collect the specimen directly into the transport fluid in the bottle, screw on the cap and dispatch. The specimen can be preserved at least for 8 days. In addition, the reagent serves to decontaminate, liquefy and concentrate the sputum. The formula for the transport medium is provided here:

Sodium chloride solution (2% w/v, aqueous) – 1000 ml

Cetylpyridinum chloride – 10 gm

Use 25 ml of the transport medium for each bottle.

8.2 Physical Examination

Physical examination includes macroscopic examination; determination of specific gravity and in some cases other physical properties.

Quantity

Normal volume of morning specimen – 2.5 ml

Normal volume of 24 hours specimens – 100 ml

Colour: The normal sputum is colourless. With infection, the sputum colour may change to yellow. Pus and epithelial cells are seen in pneumonic process.

Greenish: Due to *Pseudomonas* infection, rupture of liver abscess in lung.

Bright red: Due to recent haemorrhage, this can follow acute cardiac infarction, pulmonary infarction and pulmonary tuberculosis.

Black: Due to inhalation of dirt, cool dust or decomposition of antracotic tissue.

Rust coloured: Due to decomposition of haemoglobin seen in Pneumococcal pneumonia or Pulmonary gangrene.

Consistency and appearance: Normal sputum is colourless, watery and opalescent.

Serous: Frothy, colourless or yellow found in pulmonary oedema.

Mucoid: Glassy, tenacious, found in acute bronchitis, asthma, lobar pneumonia and whooping cough.

Purulent: Ruptured emphysema and some case of bronchiectasis.

Bloody: Mitral stenosis, pulmonary infarction, carcinoma of the lungs, pulmonary tuberculosis and acute bronchomoniliasis.

Mucopurulent: Mucous and pus found in lung cavitations and some cases of bronchomoniliasis.

Odour: Normal sputum is odourless:

(a) **Putrid:** Lung abscess, bronchiectasis and gangrene of the lung.

(b) **Sweetish:** Pulmonary tuberculosis with cavities bronchomoniliasis and bronchiectasis.

(c) **Cheesy:** Necrosis of malignant tumor and perforating emphysemas.

8.3 Simple Techniques

8.3.1 Potassium Hydroxide (KOH) Method

Aim: To examine the presence of fungus in sputum by potassium hydroxide (KOH) method.

Principle: The potassium hydroxide (KOH) preparation is ideal for determination of fungal morphology because even though, it readily dissolves the clinical materials, the fungal elements remain intact for a long period, due to the chitin in their cell wall. Gentle warming enhances the clearing effect.

Requirements

Sputum sample

Standard glasswares

10% Potassium hydroxide solution.

Procedure

1. Place a drop of 10% KOH on a clean glass slide and place the material (sputum) to be examined in the slide.
2. Place a coverslip over it. Additional KOH may be necessary and can be added at the edges of coverslip.
3. If excess, it should be removed by blotting with filter paper. Allow the preparation to stand at room temperature until it is cleared.

4. Alternatively, pass the slide quickly through a bunsen flame to accelerate clearing and expel air bubbles.
5. Observe microscopically using low intensity of light or phase contrast microscopy.

Result: White septate hyphae and conidiophores may be present.

Clinical significance: Abnormal results indicate the presence of fungus such as histoplasmosis, coccidioidomycosis or blastomycoses. Eosinophils may also be present. *Aspergillus fumigates* is commonly associated with pulmonary aspergillosis that results in granulomatous lesions in the lungs. It may complicate pre-existing lung disease like tuberculosis. *Aspergillus niger* is seen in fungal otitis in the external ear.

8.3.2 Test for Paragonimus Eggs

Aim: To examine the presence of *Paragonimus* eggs in the sputum sample.

Principle: Sputum from patients with pulmonary paragonimiasis often contains blood, mucus and stringy particles of rusty-brown gelatinous material in which masses of eggs may be found. Sputum from less heavily infected patients may contain very few eggs and concentration techniques may be necessary to detect the eggs.

Materials Required

Sputum sample

(3% w/v) Sodium hydroxide

Centrifuge

Standard glasswares

Procedure

Direct method

1. Report the appearance of the sputum—whether it is watery, mucoid, mucopurulent or jelly-like and whether it contains blood and rusty-brown particles.
2. If rusty brown gelatinous particles are present, transfer a sample of this material to a slide and cover with a

cover glass. Using a cloth or tissue, gently press on the cover glass to make a thin evenly spread preparation.

3. If no rusty brown particles are present or if no eggs are found when the particles are examined, carry out a concentration technique (preferably using sputum collected over 24 hours).

Concentration technique

1. Add an equal volume of 30 g/l (3% w/v) sodium hydroxide solution to the sputum, shake and leave for 15-30 minutes to allow sodium hydroxide to dissolve the mucus.
2. Shake well and centrifuge in a conical tube at 2000 rpm for 5 minutes. Use a plastic bulb pipette or pasteur pipette, remove and discard the supernatant fluid and transfer a drop of the sediment to a slide. Cover with a cover glass.

Note: The eggs of *Paragonimus species* are identified from knowledge of locally occurring species and by difference in egg size, shape and shell thickness.

Clinical significance: Light to moderate *Paragonimus* infections are usually asymptomatic. Heavy infections can cause pulmonary disease with inflammatory response to the flukes and eggs. Symptoms of severe pulmonary paragonimiasis often resemble those of pulmonary tuberculosis with chest pain, cough, night sweats, pleural effusion and haemoptysis (coughing up blood). *Paragonimus* flukes in the intestine and liver cause liver diseases, pain, diarrhoea and vomiting.

8.4 Staining Methods

8.4.1 Eosin Staining

Aim: To determine the presence of eosinophils in the given sputum sample by eosin staining.

Principle: Eosinophils are the granulocytic leukocyte present in the blood. The sputum has distinctive eosinophilic staining properties, which have been attributed to the increased accumulation of serum protein from the inflammation of the allergic reaction.

Materials Required: eosin, sputum sample and standard glasswares.

Preparation of reagent: Dissolve 0.1 gm of eosin in 20 ml of fresh physiological saline.

Procedure

1. Transfer a small amount of sputum to a slide and add a small drop of alkaline eosin solution.
2. Mix and cover with a cover-glass. Using the 10x and 40x objectives, with a condenser closed sufficiently to give good contrast, examine the preparation for eosinophils.

Results

Eosinophils contain bright red staining granules and a bilobed nucleus. Free eosinophilic granules may be seen in the preparation and occasionally elongated refracted charcot leyden crystals can be seen.

Clinical significance: Most cases of simple pulmonary eosinophilia are due to an allergic reaction, either from a drug such as sulphonamide or infection from a fungus or parasite *Ascaris lumbricoides*.

In bronchial asthma, the sputum is scanty, grayish white, semitransparent, viscid and tenacious containing eosinophils which are diagnostically important. Curschmann's spirals and Charcot Leyden crystals are sometimes seen.

8.4.2 Grams Staining

Aim: To differentiate bacteria into two distinctly separate groups—Gram positive and Gram negative.

Principle: Gram staining is used to determine gram status to classify bacteria broadly. It is based on the composition of their cell wall. Gram staining uses crystal violet to stain cell walls, iodine as a mordant and fuchsin or safranin as a counter stain to stain all bacteria.

Gram-positive bacteria stain dark blue or violet. Their cell wall is typically rich with peptidoglycan and lacks the secondary membrane and lipopolysaccharide layer found in Gram-negative bacteria. On most Gram-stained preparations, Gram-negative organisms will appear red or pink because they are counterstained. Due to presence of higher lipid content, after alcohol-treatment, the porosity of the cell wall increases and the CVI complex (Crystal violet-Iodine) can pass through, thus the primary stain is not retained. In contrast to most Gram-positive bacteria, Gram-negative bacteria have only few layers of peptidoglycan and a secondary cell membrane made primarily of lipopolysaccharide.

Materials Required

Crystal violet stain

Solution A

Crystal violet	– 2 gm
Ethanol	– 95% 20 ml

Solution B

Ammonium oxalate	– 0.8 gm
Distilled water	– 80 ml

Mix solution A and B and store for 24 hours before use.

Grams iodine stain

Iodine	– 1 gm
Potassium oxalate	– 2 gm
Distilled water	– 100 ml

Dissolve potassium iodide in about 50 ml of water.

Decolourizing reagent

Absolute alcohol	– 250 ml
Acetone	– 250 ml

Counterstain

Saffranine	– 0.34 gm
Absolute alcohol	– 10 ml
Distilled water	– 90 ml

Procedure

1. Cover the smear completely with crystal violet stain. Leave the slide on the stain for about one minute.
2. Pour off the stain, flood the slide with gram's iodine solution and wait for one minute.
3. Gently drain off the iodine solution and rinse with running tap water. Decolourize quickly with 95 per cent alcohol or alcohol acetone solution.
4. This decolourization process usually takes about 5 seconds. Flood the decolourization slide with counterstain saffranine. Without waiting (approximately 10 seconds) wash briefly with tap water, drain and allow to air dry.

Microscopic examination: When the slide is completely dried, first examine under low power of the objective and switch to the high power and finally to the oil immersion for higher magnification.

Result: Gram-positive bacteria stain dark blue or violet. Gram-negative organisms appear red or pink.

Clinical significance: This technique allows for morphological examination of the cells contained in the sputum and differentiates any bacteria present into either gram-positive or gram-negative organisms.

Gram staining may be used to differentiate true sputum from saliva and upper respiratory tract secretions. True sputum contains polymorphonuclear leukocytes and alveolar macrophages. It should also contain a few squamous epithelial cells. Excessive squamous cells or absence of polymorphonuclear leukocytes usually indicates that the specimen is not true sputum.

Gram staining may also provide a tentative determination of the types of leukocytes contained in the specimen. Neutrophils, which are found in infection, may be differentiated from eosinophils, characteristic of asthmatic attacks. Use of other stains such as Wright's stain can provide conclusive distinctions among types of leukocytes.

As noted, Gram-staining aids in differentiating Gram-positive from Gram-negative bacteria. Gram-staining may also be used to identify Cruschmann's spirals, which are coiled mucous filaments seen in disorders characterized by excessive mucus production accompanied by bronchial obstructions. Cruschmann's spirals are most commonly seen in asthmatic attacks, acute bronchitis and bronchopneumonia but may also be found in sputum arising from small bronchi adjacent to lung carcinoma. Fungi and other microbial parasites may also be identified by Gram-staining.

The presence of Gram-positive lancet shaped cocci, occurring singly, in pairs or in short chains suggest the infectious agent to be *Streptococcus pneumoniae*. If the Gram-negative rods are seen, it suggests *Klebsiella pneumoniae* infection. The Gram-negative pleomorphic organism is not as common but may be indicative of *Haemophilus influenzae*.

Following Romanowsky staining of the air dried smear, several other types of cells may be visible which may provide additional support for the microbiological investigations. Presence of large numbers of leucocytes suggests bacterial infections. Dust or carbon particles are seen with occupational diseases. Charcot leyden crystals (hexagonal, double pointed, slender crystals believed to be derived from eosinophils) are associated with asthma and bronchitis.

The presence of elastic tissue fibers is related to lung abscess. Patients on long-term antibiotics and steroid therapy may expectorate rounded masses (fungus balls) of *Aspergillus* that causes aspergillosis.

8.4.3 Ziehl-Neelsen Staining

Aim: To perform acid fast staining to detect the tubercle bacilli in the given sputum sample.

Principle: Organisms belonging to the genus *Mycobacterium* have a unique cell envelope that contains mycolic acid, lipids and waxes. They cannot be stained using the Gram-stain. The harsh Ziehl-Neelsen or Acid fast stain is used to stain mycobacteria. The acid fast staining method is used primarily to identify tubercle bacilli (*Mycobacterium* *tuberculosis*). Acid fast bacilli have a cell wall that resists decolourization by acid treatment; that is they will retain the stain applied to the specimen, a small portion of which is smeared on a slide, even after treatment with an acid alcohol solution.

Materials Required

1% Carbol Fuchsin reagent

25% Sulphuric acid

1% Methylene blue

Standard glasswares

Preparation of reagents

1% Carbol fuchsin

- Dissolve 5 gm of Basic fuchsin dye in 50 ml of spirit in 250 ml flask and shake well. Melt 25 gm of phenol and add it to the above solution.
- Heat the flask in water bath to dissolve the dye and make it up to 500 ml with distilled water.
- Filter the solution in a glass bottle to remove the dust particle.

25% Sulphuric acid

- Transfer 375 ml of distilled water to a 1 litre glass flask.
- Add 125 ml of concentrated sulphuric acid slowly into glass flask containing distilled water.
- Store the prepared 25 per cent sulphuric acid solution in a labelled glass bottle.

0.1% Methylene blue solution

- Add 0.5 gm of methylene blue to 1 litre glass flask containing 500 ml distilled water.
- Shake it well to dissolve and store it in a labeled glass bottle.

Staining Procedure

1. Place the slides in serial order on the slide rack with the smeared slides facing upwards. Pour 1 per cent filtered carbol fuchsin to cover the entire surface of the slide.
2. Heat the slides to steaming and leave it for 5 minutes. Then gently rinse with tap water to remove the excess carbol fuchsin. Tilt the slides to drain off excess water.
3. Pour 25 per cent sulphuric acid to the slides and allow it to stand for 2–4 minutes, till the red colour almost completely disappears from the smears.
4. Wash sulphuric acid and excess stain with tap water, make sure that the smears should not be washed away. Tilt the slides to drain off the water.
5. Pour 0.1 per cent methylene blue on slide, then allow the stain to stand for 30 seconds and gently rinse with tap water. Finally tilt the slides to drain off the water and allow it for air-drying.

Examination of Smears

Observe the slides under 100x oil immersion objective and grade as per the Table 8.1. Tubercle bacilli appear pink in colour.

Result: All bacteria or cells on the slide that are not members of genus *Mycobacterium*: Stain blue. Tubercle bacilli (*Mycobacterium tuberculosis*): Stain pink.

Sources of Error

1. Overheating (burning) during fixation can be avoided by just touching the back of the slide to the back of the hand each time the slide has been passed through the flame.
2. Do not stain smears, which have only been air-dried. Smears must also be heat "fixed".
3. After staining, it is essential that the back surface of the slide is wiped clean.
4. If washing with distilled water is not done adequately, crystallization of the stain may appear on the slide.

Clinical significance: The most common types of infections are that of the lungs by inhaling organism from the air. However, infections can also take place through contaminated food or milk from infected cows especially in children.

Disease is characterized by fever, fatigue and loss of weight. Tuberculosis may affect any organ in the body. The primary lesion is in the form of tubercles from which the infection may spread through the lymphatics to the lymph glands or through the blood to organs like the brain, spinal cord, bones, joints, kidneys or any other organ.

Since the tubercle bacillus is slow growing and culture results may take weeks, an acid fast bacillus (AFB) smear aids in early detection of the organism and timely initiation of anti-tuberculosis therapy. In addition to organisms of the *Mycobacterium genus, Nocardia* and *Actinomycetes species* may also be identified by acid fast techniques. AFB cultures are used to confirm both positive and negative results of AFB smears. By specifying that AFB is the organism to be detected on culture, the laboratory is alerted to the fact that several weeks may be needed for conclusive results. As noted, immunological methods also may be employed in diagnosing tuberculosis by sputum analysis.

Table 8.1: Grading of Microscopy Smears

Examination	Result	Grading	No. of fields to be examined
More than 10 AFB per oil immersion fields	Positive	3+	20
1-9 AFB per oil immersion fields	Positive	2+	50
10-99 AFB per 100 oil immersion fields	Positive	1+	100
1-9 AFB per 100 oil immersion fields	Scanty	Record exact number seen	100
No. AFB per 100 oil immersion fields	Negative	Negative	100

REFERENCES

Ananthanarayanan, R., 2002. *Introduction to Medical Microbiology*, Oriental Longman, New Delhi.

Craig A. Lehmann, 1998. *Sauder's Manual of Clinical Laboratory Science*, WB Saunders Company.

David Greenwood, Richard C.B. Slack and John F. Peuthere, 2002. *Medical Microbiology*, 2nd edition, Churchill Livingstone.

June, H. Cella and Juanita Watson, 2002. *Manual of Laboratory Tests*, IATBS Publishers, New Delhi.

Murray, P., E.J. Baron, J.H. Jorgensen, M.A. Pfaller and R.H. Yolken, 2003. *Manual of Clinical Microbiology*, 8th edition, Volumes 1&2, ASM Press, Washington.

9

Seminal Analysis

When a man ejaculates, the semen he expels is not made up of just sperm. Seminal fluid is also part of the ejaculatory fluid. In order for sperm to be able to fertilize an egg, it is necessary for seminal fluid to be of the correct consistency as well as for sperm to have maximum motility and ideal morphology. If any of these factors are revealed to be less than perfect in a *semen analysis*, male fertility may be compromised.

Seminal fluid components: Seminal fluid is comprised of secretions produced by the prostate gland, Cowper's gland and the seminal vesicles. All three combine to produce various types of alkaline fluids. Fluid from the prostate gland account for about 30 per cent of seminal fluid. Because of its alkaline makeup, this fluid helps to neutralize the acids naturally found in the urethra and the vagina. This prevents the sperm from being killed off on contact. The seminal vesicles produce about 60 per cent of the seminal fluids. Also an alkaline fluid, these secretions contain fructose, a type of sugar, which give sperm energy, thereby allowing them to move faster and aid them in their swim up through the uterus. The Cowper's gland along with fluid from the testes contributes the remaining fluid to the semen.

Problems with fluids: During a semen analysis, a variety of problems may be found with a man's seminal fluid. After ejaculation, male semen should liquefy within 30 seconds. If it does not, then this can indicate an infection in the seminal vesicles and prostate. Seminal fluid that is found to be too thick can make it tricky for sperm to swim through, thereby hindering conception. Thick seminal fluids can also suggest the presence of an infection in the seminal vesicles and prostate. In order to treat these two problems, semen can be processed so that live sperm is separated from the seminal fluid. This sperm can then be used in IUI.

Other problems with seminal fluids that may become apparent with a semen analysis include an absence of fructose in the semen and the wrong pH balance. If the semen collection is lacking in fructose, then a block in the ejaculatory duct is the likely problem, which can usually be treated through *surgery*. Seminal fluid that does not have an alkaline pH, a problem often associated with a low ejaculatory volume, usually indicates a problem with the seminal vesicle's functionality. Seminal fluid analysis is an important part of the semen analysis. Identifying problems with the seminal fluid can help narrow down your reasons for infertility and set you on the right path for fertility treatment.

Male infertility: Infertility due to male factor accounts for at least 40 per cent of infertility cases. For this reason, it is very important that men also be investigated for fertility problems. Male Fertility will provide you with a general overview of issues contributing to infertility in men. While blockages and problems producing healthy sperm are often the main reasons for male infertility, there are a variety of issues that can diagnosed by a fertility specialist.

Once a diagnosis has been made, a proper course of treatment can be recommended. Depending on the cause of male infertility, possible forms of treatment may include surgery, drugs or assisted reproductive technologies, like ICSI. Although infertility is often treated as a female problem, it can emotionally affect a man just as much. Regardless of whether infertility is due to male or female factor or both, men can have just as much difficulty dealing with the consequences of not being able to conceive. Learning proper coping skills can help him get through this hard time in his life.

Diagnosis male infertility: While infertility is often viewed as a female problem, the reality is that men are just as likely to account for fertility problems in a couple as women are.

Therefore, it is important that men undergo a fertility assessment when they experience troubles trying to conceive. Part of the fertility workup for men includes a semen analysis which will assess the quality of the sperm as well as look for any anti-sperm antibodies. These antibodies are detected through an assessment of the male immunology. Semen analysis can also detect whether a man is suffering from azoospermia. High levels of white blood cells in semen can also be detected by the semen analysis.

Other common tests men will likely undergo during their fertility workup include a sperm penetration assay, which evaluates how well a man's sperm can penetrate a female egg, and an acrosome reaction test. Once testing is done, there is a variety of diagnosis that a man can receive. Blood tests may show a hormonal abnormality, such as an elevated prolactin level or hypogonadism, while a current or past infection might be interfering with his reproductive system. The use of prescription drug can also significantly impact a man's fertility. Other times, there may be structural problems within a man's reproductive system. These problems can include: varicoceles, ductal abnormalities, impotence, and testicular failure.

Some men may experience retrograde ejaculation. This occurs when there are problems with the muscles or nerves surrounding the bladder neck. Also, men whose seminal fluid is too thick will likely have infertility problems as the thick fluid hinders the movement of sperm. There are a number of lifestyle factors that can affect a man's fertility. Effects of drugs and alcohol on fertility explains how the use of recreational drugs can be detrimental to your efforts in trying conceive. While we may not think about it, environmental hazards that are harmful to our fertility health are all around us.

Sample collection and delivery: The following instructions for sample collection and delivery are based on WHO recommendations. The subject should be provided with clearly written or oral instructions concerning the collection and, if required, transport of the semen sample.

- The sample should be collected after a minimum of 48 hours and no longer than 7 days of sexual abstinence.

The name of the man, period of abstinence, date and time of collection should be recorded. The time interval between the last ejaculation and sample collection should be well defined and preferentially as constant as possible in order to allow a reliable interpretation of the results of, in particular, sperm concentration and motility. When the duration of abstinence is more than 7 days, sperm motility, i.e. the proportion of spermatozoa with rapid progressive motility, may decline. If the duration of abstinence is < 48 hours, sperm concentration may be reduced, but motility will probably not be affected.

- Two semen samples should be collected for initial evaluation. The interval of time between the collections will depend on local circumstances but should not be less than 7 days or more than 3 months apart. If the results of these assessments are remarkably different, additional semen samples should be tested because marked variations in sperm output may occur within the same individual. Analysis of multiple semen specimens provides a reliable screen in the evaluation of male factor infertility. Information and support are important since semen analysis cause a moderate amount of stress.
- Ideally the sample should be collected in the privacy of a room near the laboratory. If not, it should be delivered to the laboratory within 1 hour after collection.
- The sample should be obtained by masturbation and ejaculated into a clean, wide-mouthed glass or plastic container. If plastic is used, it should be checked for lack of toxic effects on spermatozoa. The container should be warm to minimize the risk of cold shock.
- Ordinary condoms must not be used for semen collection because they may interfere with the viability of spermatozoa. In cases in which masturbation is not possible or against an individual's values, the specimen can be collected in a non-spermicidal condom

following intercourse. It has been shown that semen samples collected during intercourse using a special plastic condom or a silastic collection device tend to have better parameters. Other authors, referring to their experience, hold the view that the quality of the specimen when collected in this way is generally compromised. This way of collection should be considered for a second sample if the first one shows a relatively low volume. Coitus interruptus is not acceptable as a means of collection because it is possible that the first portion of the ejaculate, which contains the highest concentration of spermatozoa, will be lost. Moreover, there will be cellular and bacteriological contamination of the sample and the acid pH of the vaginal fluid will adversely affect sperm motility.

- Incomplete samples should be not analyzed, particularly if the first portion of the ejaculate is lost. The sample should be protected from extremes of temperature (not less than 20°C and not more than 40°C) during transport to the laboratory. The sample should be examined immediately after liquefaction and certainly within 1 hour of ejaculation.
- Laboratory technicians should be aware that semen samples may contain harmful viruses (e.g., HIV and viruses causing hepatitis and herpes) and should therefore be handled with due care.

Semen is a thick whitish secretion of the male reproductive organs discharged from the urethra on ejaculation. It contains spermatozoa or sperms, which are highly motile and mature male germ cells, which are produced by the testes and actively float in the seminal fluid. The sperm impregnates with ovum or egg during sexual reproduction. Male infertility may be due to the absence of sperms, lack of enough sperms, or defective sperms. Freshly ejaculated normal semen is highly viscous, opaque, white or silvery white in colour. A normal male ejects 2 to 5 ml of seminal fluid. Less than 1.5 ml is considered abnormal and more than 5 ml is associated with reduced fertility.

Clinical significance: Examination of the seminal fluid analysis is usually performed for infertility investigation of male. Semen analysis is first requested before the more complicated and expensive examination of the female.

9.1 Test for Sperm Count

Preparation of sperm diluting fluid (diluent): 5 gm of sodium bicarbonate mixed with 1 ml of formalin and made up to 100 ml of distilled water.

Procedure

1. Mix the specimen thoroughly by shaking gently. When seminal viscosity is markedly increased, dilute the semen with equal volume of distilled water (1:1 dilution and then the final count is multiplied by 2).
2. Take the specimen up to the 0.5 mark of WBC pipette and draw the diluting fluid up to 11 mark (1 in 20 dilution). Semen diluting fluid helps inactivates the sperms and makes them easier to count.
3. Mix well and keep it for 5 minutes.
4. Load in the haemocytometer and wait of 2 minutes to allow them to settle.
5. Count the sperms in the four corner square of the haemocytometer (as in WBC count).

Calculation

$$\text{Total sperm count} = \frac{\text{Number of sperms counted in 4 squares} \times \text{Dilution factor}}{\text{Area counted} \times \text{Depth of the chamber}} \times 1000$$

Where,

Dilution factor	:	20
Area counted	:	$4 \times 1 = 4$ sq.mm
Depth of the chamber	:	0.1 mm

Normal value: 100 to 150 million sperms/ml

9.2 Test for Motility

Active motility is must for normal spermatozoa as they to migrate from cervix to the fallopian tubes where fertilization of the ovum occurs. Based on the motility, sperm classified as follows: (i) Azoospermia—absence of spermatozoa; (ii) Oligozoospermia—only few sperms are motile; (iii) Necrozoospermia—sperms are present but immobile.

Procedure: Place a drop of semen on clean glass slide and put a cover slip over it and examine with high power objective. Count at least 200 spermatozoa. The percentage of sperms showing actual progressive motion should be recorded. Examined the slide after 3 hours and 6 hours and report the approximate number of motile sperms.

Result: If it is 80 per cent motile condition, it will be considered as normal.

9.3 Differential Sperm Count

Sperm morphology is performed by differential counts of morphologically normal and abnormal sperms.

Procedure: Place one drop of semen on a clean glass slide and make a smear and fix with methyl alcohol for one minute. Stain with diluted Giemsa stain 30 to 45 minutes and then destained with distilled water. After drying the slide, examine under oil immersion objective.

Normal: Each sperm consist of head, middle piece and tail.

Abnormal: Head too small/large or double headed. Absence of middle piece/tail or double tailed.

9.4 Test for Fructose

Fructose is the main sugar of semen. Low fructose concentration is the result of a low testosterone level.

Reagents preparation: 50 mg of resorcinol is dissolved in 33 ml of concentrated hydrochloric acid and made up to 100 ml of distilled water.

Principle: When fructose is heated with resorcinol in an acid medium, it yields a red precipitate. The reaction involves the conversion of fructose to hydroxymethyl furfural that condenses with resorcinol to form the red coloured precipitate.

Procedure: Take 5 ml of resorcinol reagent in a test tube and add 0.5 ml of seminal fluid. Bring the solution to the boil and note a colour change.

Result

Appearance of red colour precipitate within 30 seconds—Presence of fructose

No colour change—Absence of fructose.

9.5 Other Tests

Semen analysis has comparatively limited predictive value for the ability of the individual to achieve pregnancy. Additionally, 10-20 per cent of infertile couple will not have any abnormalities. In order to enhance the diagnostic power of semen analysis, new tests have been developed to identify functional defects and fertilizing potential of the sperm. The clinical data to support their use are not conclusive.

1. **Antisperm antibodies test:** Sperm agglutination, reduced sperm motility, abnormal postcoital test are suspicious for the presence of antisperm antibodies. Several tests are presently available including Sperm Immobilization test, Sperm Agglutination tests, Indirect immunofluorescence test, Enzyme-linked Immunosorbent Assay, Radiolabelled Antiglobulin Assay. Immunobead Rosette Test is one of the most informative and specific and can identified different antibody classes involved (IgG, IgA, IgM) and location on the sperm cell (head, body or tail).
2. **Computer assisted semen analysis (CASA):** Mostly for assessment of sperm concentration and specific patterns of sperm motility (velocity, linearity, etc.). The available clinical data show that the measurement obtained by CASA are correlated with conception *in vivo* and fertilization *in vitro*, but comprehensive quality control and quality assurance programs are necessary to ensure accuracy. The equipment is highly expensive.

3. **Acrosome reaction:** Absence of acrosome reaction implies poor prognosis for fertilization. The test for acrosome reaction is very expensive, labour intensive, subjective and not cost-effective since only 5 per cent of infertile patients do not demonstrate an acrosome reaction.
4. **Hamster egg penetration test:** It is to check sperm fusion ability. The diagnostic value is controversial because of difficulty in optimizing protocol. However, a zero test score may indicate a major impairment of sperm fusion capacity.
5. **Hemizona test:** In this test (to evaluate sperm zona-binding capacity) the two halves of human zona pellucida is incubated with patient's capacitated sperm and control fertile donor's sperm.
6. PCR-based detection of the pathogens in the semen in patients with asymptomatic genital infection.
7. Biochemical markers, e.g. Creatine Kinase, Reactive Oxygen Species.

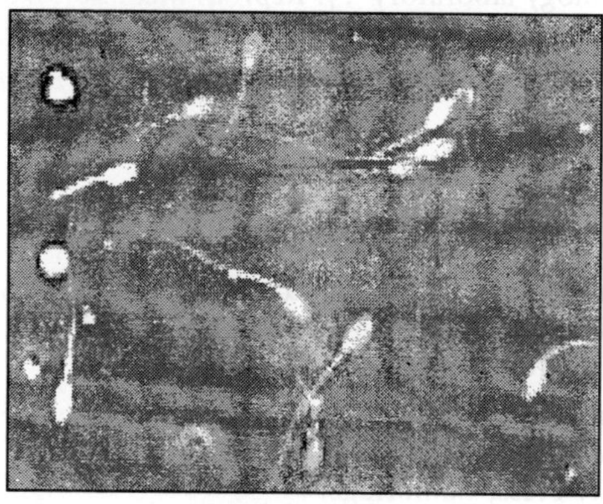

REFERENCES

Bar-Chama, N. and Lamb, D.J., 1994. Evaluation of sperm function. What is available in the modern andrology laboratory? *Urologic Clinics of North America*. 21(3): 433-46.

Bernstein, D., Tyler, J.P.P. and Driscoll, G.L., 1995. "A comparison of WHO and Tygerberg strict criteria for assessing human spermatozoa morphology". *Australian Journal of Medical Science*. 16(3): 115-17.

Chernecky, C. and Barbara, J., 2007. *Laboratory Tests and Diagnostic Procedures*. 3rd ed., Philadelphia: W.B. Saunders Company.

Comhaire, F. and Vermeulen, L., 1995. "Human Semen Analysis". *Human Reproduction*, 1, 4; 343-62.

Eimers, J.M., Omtzigt, A.M. and Vogelzang, E.T., 1997. "Physical complaints and emotional stress related to routine diagnostic procedures of the fertility investigation". *J. Psychosom Obst. Gynaecol.* 18(1): 31-33.

Irvine, D.S. and Aitken, R.J., 1994. "Seminal fluid analysis and sperm function testing". *Endocrinology & Metabolism Clinics of North America*. 23(4): 725-48.

Irvine, D.S., 1995. "Computer assisted semen analysis systems: Sperm motility assessment". *Human Reproduction*. 10(1): 53-59.

Opsahl, M.S., Dixon, N.G. and Robins, E.R., 1996. "Single vs. multiple semen specimens in screening for male infertility factors". *J. Reprod. Med.* 41(5): 313-15.

Siegel, M.S., 1993. "The male infertility investigation and the role of the andrology laboratory". *J. Reprod. Med.* 38(5): 317-34.

Sigman, M., 1993. "Laboratory testing in the evaluation of male infertility". A rational approach. *World Journal of Urology*. 11(2): 96-101.

Sofikitis, N.V. and Miyagawa, I., 1993. "Endocrinological, biophysical, and biochemical parameters of semen collected via masturbation versus intercourse". *J. Androl.* 14(5): 366-73.

WHO Laboratory manual for the examination of human semen and sperm-cervical mucus interaction. 1987. 2nd edn. Cambridge University Press, Cambridge.

WHO Laboratory manual for the examination of human semen and sperm-cervical mucus interaction. 1992. 3rd edn. Cambridge University Press, Cambridge.

10

Autoanalyzer

During the past years in clinical biochemistry there has been a considerable increase in clinical demand for laboratory investigations. When the volume of work increased, there arose a need for work simplification. Mono-step methods were introduced to replace multistep cumbersome and inaccurate methods like folin-Wu's blood sugar determination. The efficiency of mono-step methods was further increased by the introduction of automatic dispensers and diluters. For the common tests like blood glucose, blood urea, etc., however, most large laboratories found this approach still inadequate to deal with workload and instruments designed to handle the whole analytical process in a mechanized fashion have become commonplace in the last decade. This procedure is called automation. It is a self-regulating process. Where the specimen is accurate and the results are displayed in digital forms and also printed by a printer. There is an elements of feedback which detects any tendency to malfunction.

The automated instruments not only save the labour and time but also allow reliable quality control, reduce subjective errors and work economically by using smaller quantities of samples and reagents.

The various advantages of an autoanalyzer are:

1. Large number of samples can be tested in a short time.
2. Variety of tests can be performed by using various methods such as end point and rate of reaction.
3. By using techniques such as ELISA, EMIT, Chemiluminescence, Turbidimetry, Nephelometry, etc.;

it is possible to determine concentrations of hormones, drugs, tumor markers and various types of antibodies and proteins.

4. Most of the methods performed on automation are accurate, precise, sensitive and specific.
5. Automation allows laboratories to process much larger workload without a comparable increase in number of staff members.
6. Internal and external quality control programs can be implemented efficiently and effectively by using auto-analyzers.
7. In the case of fully-automated analyzers, the laboratory staff members do not come in contact with specimens and reagents (biohazardous material) and hence working on these analyzers is very safe.

Different Parts of this System

1. **Probe:** Its function was like a push-button pipette.
2. **Sampler:** This module was used to hold the batch of samples awaiting analysis in separate cups on a circular tray. This rotated at intervals.
3. **The proportioning pump:** This module determined the relative flow rates of samples and all the reagents.
4. **The dialyzer:** It contained a semi-permeable membrane and when samples were passed through it, batches of protein-free filtrate were obtained.
5. **Heating bath:** This module was used to maintain reaction mixture at a constant temperature. The batches of filtrates and reagents reacted to form coloured complexes at specified temperatures.
6. Colorimeter.
7. Printer.

Various types of Discrete Autoanalyzers

The discrete types of Auto Analyzers can be:

1. Semi-automated and

2. Fully automated
   (i) Batch analyzers
   (ii) Random access analyzers.

Semi-automated Discrete Analyzer

These analyzers are called semi-autoanalyzer, because the initial stages of a specimen analysis are performed by the laboratory technician.

Fully Automated Discrete Analyzer

These autoanalyzers perform all the functions of semi-autoanalyzers and, in addition to, that they also perform following additional functions:

- Automatic dispensing of reagents (by means of a reagent probe).
- Automatic dispensing of samples (arranged on a sampler) by means of a specimen probe.
- Automatic mixing of reaction mixtures.
- Incubating of reaction mixtures, etc.

Batch Analyzer

The autoanalyzers of this type have become outdated. These analyzers performed only one type of test at a time. There was provision to accommodate only one type of reagent at a time. These analyzers were utilized by using following general procedure:

- After collecting all the samples (particularly blood), respective sera or plasma were separated.
- Various batches of the samples were made according to the determinations such as glucose, urea, creatinine, proteins, SGPT and SGOT.
- Specific reagent was placed on the analyzer.
- The analyzer was programmed with following functions:
  (a) Pipetting of reagent in specific cups or cuvettes.
  (b) Automatic mixing of reagent and sample.

(c) Incubating of reaction mixture into the reading station, or introduction of the cuvette with the end product to the reading station.

(d) Aspiration of the reaction mixture into the reading station, or introduction of the cuvette with the end product to the reading station.

(e) Reading, calculating, displaying and printing of test results.

***Random Access Analyzers* (*RAA*)**

These analyzers perform all the functions of a batch analyzer and, in addition to that, they are equipped with:

- Random access mode (completing all tests on one sample before proceeding to the next sample).
- Sample orientation mode (completing all tests on one sample before proceeding to the next sample).
- Sequential mode (processing one test type at a time).

Compared to 'Batch' analyzers, random access analyzers are equipped with following additional facilities:

- Cuvette disk with temperature control and automatic multistage cleaning system.
- Reagent table with capacity for single or double reagent containers and facility for low temperature (8-15°C) below ambient to preserve the stability of the reagents.
- Level sensors for samples and reagents.
- Sample rack system: individual racks for samples, controls, calibrators and quality control sera.
- Facility for continuous loading of samples.
- Facility for auto-dilution.
- Plotting of daily and monthly quality control charts.
- Availability of optional ion selective electrode (ISE) module for the determination of sodium, potassium and chlorides.
- Capability to perform 2 to 3 reagents tests.

Component Steps in Fully Automated Systems

- Specimen identification.
- Specimen preparation, handling and delivery.
- Reagent handling, storage, identification and delivery.
- Mixing, incubating and reading.
- Measurement devices.
- Signal processing, handling of data and control microprocessors.

REFERENCES

Godkar, P.B. and Godkar, P.D., 2004. *Textbook of Medical Laboratory Technology*, Bhalani Publications, 2nd edition.

Marks, Vincent, Thomas Cantor, Dusan Mesko, Rudolf Pullmann, Gabriela Nosalova, 2003. *Differential Diagnosis by Laboratory Medicine*, Springer Publication.

Ochei, J. and Kolhatkar, A., 2000. *Medical Laboratory Science—Theory and Practice*, Tata McGraw Hill.

Spiegel, H., 1984. *Clinical Biochemistry, Contemporary Theories and Techniques*, Academic Press.

11

Immunodiagnostic Techniques

11.1 Ouchterlony Double Diffusion

Aim: To analyze the precipitation reactions of antigens and antibodies in gel.

Principle: Interaction between antigen (Ag) and antibody (Ab) at the molecular level forms the basis for several techniques that are useful in modern day scientific studies and in routine clinical diagnosis. These techniques are either based on the use of labelled reagents, a tracer or immunoprecipitation. Ouchterlony double diffusion (ODD) or double immunodiffusion technique is one of the simplest techniques extensively used to check antisera for the presence of antibodies for a particular Ag and to determine its titre.

In ODD assays, solutions of Ag and Ab are placed in adjacent wells cut in agarose gel and are allowed to diffuse radially. The Ag and Ab concentrations are relatively higher near their respective wells. As they diffuse farther from the wells, their concentration decreases. An antigen will react with its specific antibody to form an Ag-Ab complex. At one point their concentrations become equivalent and the Ag-Ab complex precipitates to form a precipitin line.

Materials Required

Immunodiffusion kit: agarose, 10x assay buffer, antigen, test antiserum, glass plate, gel punch with syringe and template.

Standard glasswares: conical flask, measuring cylinder, test tubes, distilled water, micropipette, tips, moist chamber.

Procedure

1. Boil to dissolve 100 mg of agarose in 10 ml of 1x assay buffer, cool to 55°C.
2. Pour 5 ml of the gel solution onto clean glass plate placed on a horizontal surface. Allow the gel to set; it takes approximately 20-30 minutes.
3. Place the gel plate on the template provided. Punch wells in the gel with the help of a gel punch corresponding to the markings on the template. Use gentle suction to avoid forming rugged wells.
4. Serially dilute the test antiserum up to 1:32 dilution as follows:
   (a) Take 20 μl of 1x assay buffer in each of the five vials.
   (b) Add 20 μl of test antiserum into the first vial and mix well.
   (c) The dilution of antiserum in this vial is 1:2.
   (d) Transfer 20 μl of 1:2 diluted antiserum from the first vial into the second vial.
   (e) The dilution in this vial is 1:4.
   (f) Repeat the dilutions up to fifth vial as shown in figure.
5. Add 10 μl of the antigen to the centre well and 10 μl each of neat (undiluted), 1:2, 1:4, 1:8, 1:16, 1:32 dilutions of antiserum into the surrounding wells as shown in figure.
6. Place the plate in a moist chamber and incubate overnight at room temperature.
7. After incubation, observe for opaque precipitin line between the antigen and antisera wells.
8. Note down the highest dilution at which the precipitin line is formed. This is the titre value of the antiserum. A typical ODD pattern of low titre antisera is given in the figure.

Observation

Antisera dilutions in well 1-6: (1) Neat, (2) 1:2, (3) 1:4, (4) 1:8, (5) 1:16, (6) 1:32, (7) the centre will contain antigen.

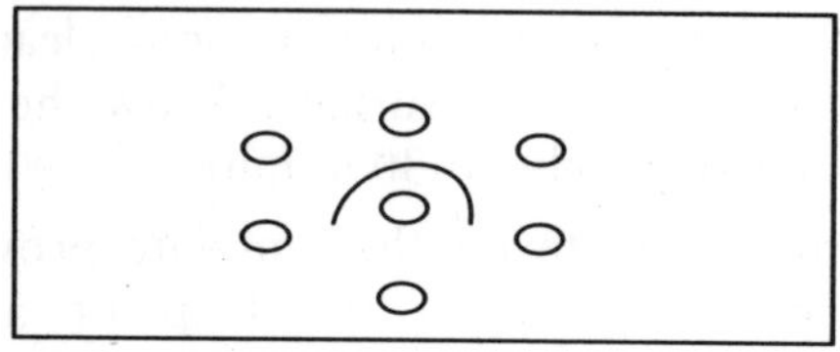

11.2 HCV Elisa Test

Principle: HCV test kit is a third generation ELISA for the detection of antibodies against HCV in human serum or plasma. Microwells are coated with HCV specific recombinant antigens from the putative C-core (structural), E1 and E2 (Envelop proteins), NS3, NS4 and NS5 (nonstructural) regions of HCV genome. It has been observed that recombinant antigens obtained from a single genotype of the virus is not sufficient to detect the anti-HCV antibodies in all cases. In this assay, diluted serum samples are incubated in microwells coated with a cocktail of specific recombination HCV antigens.

After washing, to remove the excess serum and unbound antibodies, the captured anti-HCV antibodies are incubated with enzyme peroxidase conjugated anti-human IgG and this complex is detected by adding chromogen (TMB) and H_2O_2 as substrate. The appearance of blue colour in microwells indicates the presence of anti HCV antibodies. This reacmineral acid, resulting in a yellow colour, which is measured at a wavelength of 450 nm in a ELISA reader with 630 nm is the reference filter.

Requirements

HCV ELISA test kit: Reagent–1 Sample diluent, Reagent–2 Conjugate, Reagent–3 Washing buffer, Reagent–4 Negative control, Reagent–5 Positive control, Reagent–6 Colour reagent, Reagent–7 Stopping solution, Reagent–8 Microwell strips, Adhesive strip covers.

Standard glasswares: Double distilled water, multi-channel pipette 100 μl, micro pipette 20–200 μl and 100–1000 μl, disposable tips, automatic dispensing washer, measuring cylinder 100 ml, timer, disposable absorbent pad or towels, disinfectants, disposable gloves, bichromatic microplate ELISA reader.

Reagent Preparation

Preparation of washing buffer: Dilute the concentrated washing buffer 1:10 with distilled or reagent grade water. 500 ml of diluted buffer is sufficient to wash all the 96 wells. If all the strips are not to be used at a time, prepare proportionate amount of washing buffer. All other reagents are supplied as ready to use.

Others: Blank, positive and negative controls must be included with each run. All liquid reagents must be gently mixed before use. Colour reagent (reagent 6) consists of substrate and chromogen, is ready to use and needs no preparation. Before addition, all reagents should be brought to room temperature.

Sample collection: Clear, non haemolysed serum or plasma can be used. Specimen/samples can be stored at 2–8°C upto 4 weeks or at –20°C or lower for long-term storage. Use of fresh and non heat inactivated samples is preferred. Grossly haemolysed or contaminated samples should not be used.

ELISA reader: ELISA plate washers and readers are to be operated as per specifications of the manufacturers. Pipette used should be regularly calibrated so as to dispense exact volume of reagents specified, and prevent loss of extra reagents.

Procedure

1. Take out required number of microwell strips (reagent 8) to perform the test and label the wells approximately. Remaining strips, along strips, along with absorbent should be kept in the pouch provided for the purpose.
2. Add 200 µl of sample diluent (reagent 1) to control and test wells of the microwell strips (reagent 8) except blank well. Leave the blank well empty.

3. Add 10 µl of negative control (reagent 4) to 1B, 1C and 1D and 10 µl of positive control (reagent 5) to 1E and 1F. To rest of the wells, add 10 µl of sample.
4. Mix properly and cover the microwells with adhesive strip covers provided and allow to stand at room temperature (20-30°C) for 30 minutes.
5. Remove and discard the adhesive strip covers. Decant the content of the wells into a waste container. Fill the wells with approximately 350 µl of diluted washing buffer (reagent 3) and allow soak time of 30 seconds per well (program the auto washer for soak time of 30 seconds) and then decant it in the waste container. Repeat for 4 more times. Drain wells on a disposable absorbent pad or towel and tap firmly to remove excess of fluid. Take care not to scratch the inner surface of the well with pipette tips or tissue paper (add the next reagent immediately after washing and tapping).
6. Add 50 µl of conjugate (reagent 2) to each microwell except 1A i.e. (reagent 2) blank well. Mix the contents of microwells by agitating the strips gently for 5–10 seconds and cover the strips with fresh adhesive strip covers.
7. Incubate at room temperature for 30 minutes and then remove and discard the adhesive strip covers.
8. Wash each microwell, 5 times, as instructed in step 4.
9. Tap microwells on a fresh disposable absorbent pad or towel and tap firmly to remove all moisture present in the wells. Take care not to scratch the inner surface of microwells with pipette tips or tissue paper (add next reagent immediately after washing and tapping).
10. Add 100 µl of colour reagent (reagent 6) to all the microwells including blank well. Cover with fresh adhesive strip covers.
11. Incubate at room temperature for 30 minutes (place the plate in dark, away from direct light).

12. Remove and discard adhesive strip covers and add 100 µl of stopping solution (reagent 7) to all the microwells to stop the reaction.
13. Mix the contents of the microwells by agitating the tissue gently for 5–10 seconds.
14. Read results in either monochromatic (450 nm) or bichromatic (450–630 nm) mode. Absorbance readings must be taken after blanking with A1 well (Reagent Blank). Take readings within 30 minutes of addition of stopping solution.

Calculation (Cut off Value)

The cut off value is calculated based on the mean absorbance of 3 negative controls and addition of a factor (0.225) i.e.

$$NC\overline{X} = \frac{NC_1 + NC_2 + NC_3}{3}$$

Cut off value = NCX + 0.225

Interpretation of Results

All samples with absorbance less than cut off value should be considered non reactive for HCV. Samples with absorbance more than cut off value should be considered reactive and positivity should be confirmed by retest. For confirmation of reactive samples, it is advisable to retest all samples in duplicate, by the same procedure as described above. If one or both of the supplicate samples give positive result, the sample is confirmed as reactive.

Limitation of the Test

Positive samples are to be retested in duplicate. If the value is consistently equal to or greater than cut off value the results must be confirmed by another acceptable similar or confirmatory test. Like other diagnostic tests, a definite clinical diagnosis should be avoided on results of a single test. A complete evaluation by physician is mandatory. A non reactive result with this test also does not preclude the possibility of HCV infection.

11.3 HIV ELISA Test

The epidemiological evidence indicates that an infectious agent transmitted through intimate contact, intravenous drug use or use of infected blood or blood products leads to acquired immunodeficiency syndrome (AIDS). This disease affects T cell mediated immunity, resulting in severe lymphopenia and a reduced subpopulation of helper T lymphocytes. Destruction of this T lymphocytes population by the virus causes an immune deficiency resulting in a reduced or deficient response to subsequent infections. Consequently infections become more severe and may cause death. At present, there is no successful treatment for AIDS.

The etiological agent has been identified as a retrovirus, human immunodeficiency virus type 1 (HIV–1). A closely related, but distinct second type of immunodeficiency virus, designated HIV–2, has been isolated and cause a disease that is indistinguishable from AIDS. Serological cross-reactivity between HIV–1 and HIV–2 has been shown to be highly variable from sample to sample. This variability necessitates the inclusion of antigen to both HIV–1 and HIV–2 for the detection of antibodies to HIV–1 and HIV–2.

Principle: The test is based on non competitive "sandwich" ELISA. HIV recombinant protein antigens gp–41, C terminal of gp–120 and gp–36 (a peptide) representing the immunological regions of HIV–1 and HIV–2 envelope genes are immobilized. Test sample is added to the microtitre well and coated with recombinant HIV–1 and HIV–2 antigens. If HIV antibody is present in the test sample, it binds to the antigens coated on the microwell. After washing the microwell to remove unbound antibody, protein A–horseradish peroxidase conjugate is added, which binds to the antibody to form antigen–antibody–conjugate complex. Unbound conjugate is removed by subsequent washing. MB substrate is then added to the microwell and incubated. In the presence of antigen–antibody–conjugate complex, the colourless TMB substrate is hydrolysed by horseradish peroxidase to form a blue colour end product. Addition of the stop solution leads to yellow colour which is read at 450 nm. The method is easy to perform and is very reliable. Controls are also provided to eliminate false results.

Requirements

HIV kit: microtitre plate, dilution buffer, wash solution, TMB substrate, positive control, negative control, HRP conjugate (concentrated 100x), HRP conjugate diluent, stop solution, adhesive slips, standard glasswares.

Reagent Preparation

1. Bring all reagents and microtitre wells to room temperature (20–30°C) before running the assay.
2. Gently mix all liquid regents before use.
3. Dilute the wash solution 1:10 with distilled water or deionized water, diluted wash solution stored at 2–8°C is stable for two weeks, if the concentrated wash solution shows any crystals dissolve them by warming in a water bath at 37°C before dilution.
4. Preparation of working HRP conjugate-dilute 100x HRP conjugate 1:100 with HRP conjugate diluent as required for e.g. for 8 wells use 10 μl 100x HRP conjugate and 1 ml of HRP conjugate diluent.

Procedure

1. Set up the microtitration wells in the frame provided and label each well. Label one well as reagent blank and two wells each as positive and negative controls.
2. Add 200 μl of ready to use dilution buffer into required number of wells.
3. In duplicate, add 20 μl of positive and negative controls to appropriately labelled wells of the microtitre plate.
4. Add 20 μl of test sample into appropriately labelled well and mix thoroughly by gentle swirling.
5. Cover the wells with foil or adhesive slips.
6. Incubate at RT for 30 minutes (20–30°C).

7. Aspirate and dispose the samples along with microtips into a container containing 0.5 per cent sodium hypochlorite (ordinary bleach).
8. Wash the microplate 5 times with approximately 300 μl per well of working solution. Care should be taken to avoid overfilling and cross contamination.
9. Add 100 μl of working HRP conjugate solution to each well in the same order.
10. Incubate at RT for 30 minutes (20–30°C).
11. Wash the microplate 5 times with approximately 300 μl per well of working solution.
12. Add 100 μl of ready to use TMB substrate solution to each well in the same order.
13. Incubate at RT for 30 minutes (20–30°C) in dark (avoid exposure to light).
14. Stop the reaction by adding 2 drops (approximately 100 μl) of the stop solution to each well in the same order.
15. Read the absorbance at 450 nm ELISA reader within 10 minutes.

Test Validity

Two negative and two positive controls must be included on each run. The control results must be explained before the interpretation of sample results. Absorbance of single well blank must be lesser than 0.150. Absorbance if individual negative control values must be lesser than or equal to 0.250. The positive control mean absorbance must be greater than or equal to 1.200. If the mean value of positive control is less than 1.200 the run should be repeated.

Calculations

The cutoff value is calculated by multiplying the average absorbance value of HIV Positive control by 0.1 and adding the average absorbance value of negative control.

Cutoff value = (0.1 × PC) + NC

PC = Positive control

NC = Negative control

Interpretation of Results

1. Specimens with absorbance values less than the cutoff value are considered non-reactive by the HIV ELISA test and may be considered for antibodies negative for antibodies to HIV–1/2. Further testing is not required.
2. If the values are 10 per cent less or more than the cutoff value, then the samples must be retested.
3. Specimens with absorbance values equal to or greater than the cut off value are considered initially reactive by the HIV–1/2 ELISA. The original sample should be retested (in duplicate) before final confirmation of the result.
   (a) Initially reactive specimens that do not react in either of the duplicate, repeated tests are considered negative for antibodies to HIV–1/2. Further testing is not required.
   (b) Initially reactive specimens that react in either or both of the duplicate, repeated tests are considered repeatably reactive for antibodies to HIV–1/2.
4. If the specimen is repeatably reactive, the probability of antibodies to HIV–1/2 is high, especially with patients at high risk for infection or with very high absorbance values. In most settings, it is appropriate to investigate repeatable reactive specimens by supplemental testing, such as western blot, immunofluorescence or radio-immunoprecipitation. The interpretation of results of specimens found repeatably reactive by ELISA and negative on additional more specific testing is unclear, further clarification may be obtained by testing another specimen three to six months later.

Limitations of the Procedure

AIDS and other HIV-related diseases are clinically diagnosed that can only be established by a physician. The HIV–1/2 ELISA kit alone cannot be used to diagnois AIDS, even if the recommended investigation of reactive specimens suggests a high probability that antibody to HIV is present. A negative test result does not preclude the possibility of exposure to or infection with HIV. Data obtained from testing populations at increased risk and at low risk for HIV antibodies suggest that repeatable reactive specimens are more likely to demonstrate the presence of HIV antibodies with supplemental testing, such as western blot, immunofluorescence or radioimmunoprecipitation. Reactivity at or only slightly above the cutoff value is more frequently non-specific from persons at low risk for HIV infection.

REFERENCES

John Bernard Henry, 2001. *Clinical Diagnosis and Management by Laboratory Methods*. W.B. Saunders Publication, 20th edition.

Kanai L. Mukherjee, 2002. *Medical Laboratory Technology—A procedure manual for routine diagnostic tests*, Tata McGraw Hill Publishing, 11th edition.

Manual of Basic Techniques for a Health Laboratory, 2005. World Health Organization, III edition, New Age International Publishers.

Monica Cheesbrough, 1998. *District Laboratory Practice in Tropical Countries*, Part I, Cambridge University Press.

Praful B. Godkar and Darshan P. Godkar, 2003. *Textbook of Medical Technology*, III edition, Bhalani Publications.

Ramnik Sood, 2002. *Medical Laboratory Technology—Methods and Interpretation*, Brother Publications, V edition.